Society

The World in Which We Live

Jonathon Nazario

Contents

I would like to thank the people who had a helping hand in making this book a reality:

Dad: Thank you for developing the proper mindset within me and for creating an environment in which we can talk, not just as father and son but as people.

Mom: You have done so much for me, you have set my attitude and made sure balance was always at the forefront of your mind.

Friends: You have all helped me in this endeavor from all of your unique qualities, whether it was your brutal honesty, your audible support or even just listening, you guys have all had an impact on me and I thank you for making me who I am today.

Moreira Family: This family did not do me a favor because of who I am but they did it because of their message. Help anyone that asks and give them the 100% they deserve on the condition they do it for someone else. They want kindness to ripple through the ocean of humanity so I wish to promote it not only because it's the right thing to do but because I believe in this message as well. After all, it's why we have two hands.

Introduction

You are a hypocrite. But more importantly, this space is for the book, not you, no matter how much you want "five steps to live better." The reality is you won't find this here or anywhere. The only way to get from point A to point B is to put in the effort like everyone else and claim the desired output. But everything is a choice, here at 16, I hear people and teenagers alike saying they have a problem and do not know what to do. The first thing I ask them is if they are willing to put forth the effort, and just like someone desperate, they blatantly agree until they hear the reality of what it takes. All I hear afterward is silence followed by rejection and denial as if they just got sent to Hell on accident and they need to speak with customer service on a return.

Whenever something bad happens, they always give their sympathies in words rather than actions. If you are on your phone asking for something to be done, all you'll hear is, "I understand, and I am sorry." Like a broken record on repeat, but when they do their job and help, it is a godsend. Imagine if your Amazon driver only delivered half the packages they grabbed, to return them at the end of the day, to maybe get to yours tomorrow.

Everyone has a goal that they want to achieve, but there are only a couple of differences between you and the upper echelon of society. The most important one being staying active, not tomorrow, but today. The time at which you do something is significantly less important than actually doing it. So, the next time you think about getting a beach body, start doing the work now knowing the amount does not matter. Just the sheer act of starting will make it harder to stop since your brain does not like leaving things unfinished; it likes closure.

Growing up, there may come a time when a teacher makes a mistake, but everyone stays silent because it's the teacher, and everyone is afraid they might be wrong. Then one brave soul raises their hand and points out the mistake, and everyone says, "Yeah, I thought that too." Let's say society is the teacher, in this case, and successful people are the brave souls altering the class learning. Not every time they think a mistake is made it will mean they're correct, so society goes back and explains why it is what it is. Welcome to Society.

If we focus on reality, you are just a rabbit drawn along with a carrot on a stick. Not to say evolution has failed us, but our biology is continuously in the past, just like our law system with no way to get ahead. But everything has its proper context; fear of risk is an everyday fear that needs to be abolished, within reason. Again, I'm not saying to gamble at Vegas as your nine to five job but the calculated risk can be the most beneficial thing of your life; it is one thing to jump off a bridge and another to jump off knowing that there is a good chance of landing safely. Now, most people will be in the same position as you at some point in your life, but acknowledging the risks and educating oneself can lead to more in-depth analysis and better decision making. This book will be just one stepping stone in the creation of your new self-image, and on how you decide to make choices in everyday scenarios and critical situations.

People only tell you things for three reasons: to acknowledge, to do something, or to pass time. Now, deciding and labeling your conversations based on the level of importance can help sort out your priorities. Helping differentiate between conversations to further your goals and those made from lack of loneliness. Though what controls and compels us is not money or items, but rather time, the resource we always have but can never get enough of and is never promised to last but it's expected for there to be more of. Based on these concepts, I will shape your mind and the thought process of yourself, hopefully creating an eye-opening and enlightening series through storytelling and the oh so dull sciences. But you guys hit the jackpot personality-wise, with graceful sarcasm and enigmatic riddles that could be harder to decrypt then your passwords: "pass, password, or 1234."

Legend

The muscles of practicality and the muscles
of the theoretical,
Are two worlds so different yet people focus
on the opposite,
Is it just me,
Or is reality, only a false facade,
No matter how much it gets covered,
With the happiness and the parties,
You and I are still here,
Not there,
Why lie,
We all seek the truth yet we all cover it,
We say something...
But mean something completely different,

We are mixed signals in the handbook of prior communication.

Why are we here?
I know we look but when we find our answer we just cover it,
Surrounded by media of all sorts,
Giving us examples of ourselves,
But it will not happen because we are us,
It will not happen because it is me,
Just because it is a small chance for something to happen,
Does it mean it is impossible?
Lightning can strike the same place twice.

So believe it, prepare for the worst case, find the best can happen,
The sight you see when you close your eyes is the goal,
Aim for it;
Everyone misses,
Get up and try again,
There are times when breaks are needed, but excuses are not,
That is the reason you are here,
Try to meet the expectation,
Whether you do it at eighteen or sixty,
It makes no difference.

But once you "make it,"
Form a new goal, there is no end goal for people like us,
We keep grabbing and reaching till it goes black,
Nothing stops the unstoppable;
There are setbacks,
Nothing stops you,
They can try,
And they may think that it works,
You have infinite torque but applying it rather than sitting and spinning is the difference,
Mistakes in the past were points of learning, not regret,
Do not make the same one twice,
It will be too expensive to cover a second time.

The people with the most money are not the wealthiest,
You decide your wealth and whatever you choose,
Whether rich or poor,
It just needs to be yours, not the big man upstairs,
Standing tall yet only standing,
Threatening but never enforcing,
Just a figment of a self-image.

Everything is a transaction. It does not matter what you are doing or who you are doing it with; it just is. So why you of all people? Odds are, they will win more or lose less, but it does not mean you have to be at the "losing" end, which is what presumably happens to you a lot. Here is a fun fact; not everyone wants to waste their time in a conversation even though it is a transaction. When was the last time you thought about what you did or why you did it? Let me use the concept of lying as an example to make it easier; the average adult lies every ten minutes, but that is not you, right? You are above lying, and it feels good to lie to yourself. But any action that feels good we are bound to repeat in the future, which means younger generations will rely on this more than the previous generation for that simple reason.

What more could one want than to feel great? What is more significant than satisfaction? Do you even know why we like what we like? One day I was off looking at social media and found an oddly satisfying video, as you do. I wondered what made it so enjoyable and so I did some research. I came up with the idea that "perfection" is the satisfaction we seek and feel because it's "too perfect" for us. We know we will not be able to obtain anything close to that level, a feeling almost the same as the one we get when someone accomplishes a goal or something similar. Perfection is what we, as a society, strive for but continuously fail to maintain. However, in life, nothing is black and white. Society attempts to plan for chaos even though it works best when perfection is in our midst, which is never, by the way. But society does not intend for the havoc; it plans for entropy, and the difference in your mind is probably that they are similar. Although chaos is disorder, along the lines of anarchy and entropy it's randomness and pure randomness with all connotations aside. Sure it is easy to prepare and account for the perfect world, but what happens when it is absent as it always is, or something happens that is out of your control, entropy ensues no matter the scale. We will be going into this later, but for now, let me shine a little light on personal imperfection and what happens when something does not go our way. We get annoyed and, most of the time, mentally quit on the task at hand, but the reason we live life is because of the unknown and the possibility that you can do anything you desire, yet few do.

Measurements are an exciting thing, primarily when you think about whether we discovered them or if we created them. Most see it as an argument, yet both sides have their accuracies. People have debates over issues and how things should be a certain way. Yet, the only way something gets done is if there is some sort of compromise involved in the situation, it is generally the best and most logical scenario. In most cases, people see it as one or the other, kind of like a multiple choice question with two options, but the ones that think outside the box are the ones that can get things done. Almost every argument has a black and white answer, yet most fall in the gray areas; it all depends on whether we look through the lens of life or the ideal world.

Haven't you ever wondered why there is no generally accepted pain system, and it is not because they lack volunteers, which is unusual? (There are a lot of people out there willing to go through pain for this kind of study) Moreso, it was the fact that scientists could not find an accurate measurement of pain since it is relative to the individual, but we can all agree that getting slammed in the *pelotas* is painful? Which for any of you mono linguists out there, which I call Americans, it means balls in Spanish. The power of relativity is something we will cover as people do not realize just how different something can indeed be.

I want you to think about a logistical system, for more of a challenge, think of a metro or subway system like the MTA (Metropolitan Transport Authority) where you cannot just shift into a different lane. It is a pretty impressive feat,

13

especially if it is an efficient and cost-effective system. But who knows what is hard for you because everything is relative even the sun. It is the center that is relative to the solar system and the United States is west of the Atlantic. Still, if you look from the pacific ocean, it becomes east along with China, and all the other Asian countries are the new west. Something exciting is the notion that we might have to add Earth to our address one day, now there's a crazy thought. The longer I live, the more I seem to notice the fact that nothing is simple in life. If we look at the U.S. power grid, you would assume it would be one system, and that would be wrong. Now, if you think there would be one for each of the time zones, I would agree, for that's a pretty good thought process, but you only got it half right. It turns out there are three power grids, but it is one for the eastern seaboard, one for the western seaboard, and one for Texas. Yes, just Texas, oddly enough, I would assume it is due to Texas' crude oil production and use of power to sustain the local area, but, as you should know, Texas is a massive state.

Another thing that may be considered unusual is why individual states are the size they are. Have you ever thought about it, you notice for the most part the further west you go the more significant states get (in size), and there are only two reasonable explanations for this. Número Uno, their size must have been based on fundamental environmental issues, the people at the time would not have had the resources or skills to advance. Or the fact that technology evolved causing states to be more significant in size because it was faster to go between places, but those are only my ideas, and we will go further in-depth to the reasoning and potential theories later down the line. Scary fact, if you did not already know, most, if not all, United States cities only have two weeks' worth of food to supply a town, so in the unlikely event of a disaster, some of you are loving me now. We could very quickly go hungry and lose ourselves and our minds in the face of starvation. We could very well pull one out of the history books and make do like The Starving Time in Jamestown, where they would eat leather and other such items.

In this book, I will transform your ideas, thoughts, and beliefs, but during it, you will most likely not even notice your behavior change, but the family you see once a year will think you have changed for the better, assuming they are not Karen. Reading this is supposed to be like going to the gym, you cannot pinpoint the day at which the results happened, but you are aware of yourself before, and now you will see and feel the after as well as the compelling story it tells. When convincing people you need to treat it like playing darts with each one being your prescription of healing their idiocy, some might not work, and you just need to try till you get that bullseye to change their views. Psychology affects everyone (just about) and is continuously changing people, especially with an environment like the one in our modern-day society. The important thing about this is that it works no matter if you believe it or not. Although making yourself aware of it can help you implement it and notice it, allowing for you to not fall into the pitfalls most do, because you are not most and if you are now. You will not be when I am done with you.

As you can tell, I believe everyone should have the opportunity to learn about themselves to improve themselves, but I am not talking about taking a class. Because odds are they will not tell you anything significant other than the history of it and the politically correct term. This was the case with Advanced Placement Psychology where I knew the effects and how to implement them past what they taught me. But I did not know what the consequences or the people were called/named, making it relatively useless when I went through it as I did not care for the people that coined the effects. Still, the teacher was a legend. Just now, a thought is causally passing my mind, but to exfoliate on the point I am attempting to make because I am having way too much fun with this. Stare at someone's ankle, but before you go off and close the book and try it, please read the "fine print" written after this. Note, you must do this while in a conversation, or when they are looking at you, it will make them feel weird and insecure, causing them to "hide" their ankles, thus putting a lot of stress on said person. But they do need to acknowledge your presence for best results, and it would be in your best interest not to do this to someone you do not know, as I could see this as an arrestable offense. It can be a lot of fun to do it to the opposite gender. Now that I think about it, I hope none of these points overlap at any given moment, even though it is bound to happen.

One word relevance, but so many people can not account for it because in life there will always be people better than you and people worse than you in anything yet the way we work is to aim for the top, a little ironic. You will eventually be familiar with the definition of insanity as it is doing the same thing over and over again and expecting a different outcome. So far, it seems like my writing, but hey, this is from my point of view. I believe this is one of the critical problems with my generation. We expect success to come easy, but if you base yourself on our society, it is the results that matter rather than direct effort. I do not care who you are; do not try to talk about a topic you are not familiar with when someone is attempting to learn it. Those people need to learn a lesson my father taught me,

"Only speak if you have something of value to add." My generation has issues; it's like we only have fifteen hours a day compared to the twenty-four everyone else has. Everyone says they are too busy, but you can shave off time on everyday activities little by little, but we don't understand that it adds up. Or if you spend your time doing productive things, most likely you will be spending some of this time doing non-productive things such as texting while driving. But the good thing about people in our society is that ordinary people only work, and truly work, three hours a day which means we are technically working less than half the time we are at our jobs so we could globally increase production by over fifty percent according to math. Still, it would probably look more like thirty percent because people are lazy and this average may not be completely accurate.

Learning is a process, but one we learn to hate, and it is not because it is inherently tricky. Although, it is due to how we learned it when we were young; we associate learning with school when in reality they are separate, but due to this "trauma" at such a young age, we create this negative mindset towards it. School is one of those things where I believe in the system, just not the people who run it. The concept is excellent; you drop your irresponsible kids off and tell them some of the information needed to live. Sure, the core subjects are necessary, but have we ever looked at it with a magnifying glass? Our schools across the nation are continually pulling money from future school years, at this point. To say, "I'll pay it back later, when we get more money" but enough about that for now.

What we are learning is relatively invalid; it seems evident that we should be graded on a bell curve, meaning one person always gets a zero and one gets a one hundred no matter what because it would make the classroom more competitive. Everyone knows friendly competition is favorable for almost everyone involved, and we can see this within companies such as AMD and Intel. The two primary central processing unit (CPU) brands and it provided massive leaps in performance over recent years because they were both fighting for the same market share. Not to get into any thoughts about this now, but they are both still engineering feats that compete for the same market share. But if we translate this competition into our modern-day classroom we would learn that resources are our limiting factor and nothing else. Everything is based on limiting factors and not unlimited ones like money. Still, it would make the failing grade a twenty percent to compensate, compared to the usual fifty. Since we cannot all get A's in life, work hard, and it will have its own reward.

I am here to greet the book you know as Society properly. From this point forward, there will be operative paragraphs and more poor life choices. It is okay. At least they are mine, and as we have already established, I do not know anything according to society. So let us follow the yellow brick road of life where some of us try to meet our goals and others do not wish to "sweat" in life. Yes, there will be a language that is outside of standard English in this book, so I recommend you open that Urban Dictionary as you read this, this is a note for Boomers and the "uncultured."

But since you have already looked at the table of contents, let me explain to you my perspective and the reason I wrote the first chapter as I did; every paragraph mentions something vaguely crucial, and yes, that is supposed to be oxymoronic. If you think about any of these points on either a surface level or on a deeper level, you will see that there will be two different messages, although one is generally more evident than the other. And since you can live your life the way you want, you can choose if this is a waste of time or not, you decide your take away as I will try my best to explain the more profound reason that you may not have even thought about yet, although I can only do so much. But as you go through every paragraph, you will realize the beginning correlates to a chapter of this book and some to multiple sections, nothing new in this genre, I hope. Still, there will be profound messages with sarcasm of the funny kind.

Also, do not forget my best friend called controversy; he always is felt but never heard. I highly doubt that you will agree with all of my points, but even if you walk away with one thing learned or implemented, I will be happy. During this, I will also be including my own experience to give this book a soul because I am not sure my vibrant personality is enough. More importantly, you landed on, "Book format, if you happen to get bored of any of this, please skip to chapter two satisfaction." But you would not do it in a movie or tv show unless you are one of those people; I recommend reading everything you never know what secrets lie off the beaten path.

But, for every three chapters, there is a common topic, and each one builds into the next, by the way, chapter five through seven is where it is at for sure, just saying. I know you are wondering how some of the stuff from earlier ties into a one-word topic but it does, trust me. I would say everything here is necessary, whether you agree with me or not. Maybe just the thought of what I say can activate cognitive dissonance and for those of you that are too narcissistic to be taking advice from a sixteen-year-old; hey, you guys get to say age is only a number. So treat it this way for all circumstances. Not just the handpicked ones or I might have to refer you to the "Introduction" of the book since it seems a little redundant to waste my valuable words explaining what is already stated. Also, for everyone, including that narcissistic guy, cognitive dissonance, "Is the state of having inconsistent thoughts, beliefs, or attitudes, especially when relating to behavioral decisions and attitude adjustments" (Shout out to Google). Which, in turn, creates an internal battle till you sort out your inner demons, basically like mental chakras, for those of you that are into that.

Interestingly I took that hypothetical person and made it a male rather than a gender-neutral person; I wonder what that says about me. On a more realistic note for when someone is reading this in the future, they may not know what Google is or how it works even though it seems like common knowledge now, with some saying how could anyone not know what Google is. The same thought could be said about the beeper or pager, but if you have kids or you are currently a kid. You will realize that you do not know what beeper is or you will think back to the time when memories were in black and white because yes that's how that worked; all of you Zoomers just, believe me, as someone who has not even had direct experience with it. But overall it is so inconsequential to life that your parents will most likely never explain it to you. So as this book gets shot off into history, I would like to kind of future proof it and make it understandable to everyone who wants to read it from kids to the elderly, in any other English-speaking country.

For those that do not travel much, traditions, customs, and systems are very different from their reality at home. What I mean by this is that things that seem natural to you are just that, natural to you, more people are reading than you, so if it seems a little redundant do not get frustrated but take it as a learning opportunity for conversation. So that when you are talking with someone who is statically different from you, you can make such changes to confirm they know what you are talking about. Compared to them thinking about the "normal" way to look you in the eyes as you talk in what appears an endless time loop of words to the point where they are not even sure if you guys are both speaking the same language.

Just because I want to, "the make or break chapter" will be a little bit longer, I will further talk about this book as a whole. The majority of the life lessons in this are ones I believe more people need to hear, but we do need to keep in mind that I am only a naive teenager; what do I know? That line is going to be repeated because, for sure, the vast majority of us are not mentally gifted with being functional adults, but there are always those special snowflakes. Although, I risk being labeled as egomaniacal by giving myself praise, heavens no. But overall I do need to say this over and over again as annoying as it may be, it stands as a precaution to anything I say and shows how much or little I have done in this part of my life, but mainly the latter. The reason anything I say about myself comes with a positive note and then a dropkick is to represent the volatility of today's media. Anything you say can be taken out of context and everything will be if you are important enough. Now to break the fourth wall, which is what I believe I am up to, this part is meant to show what you can learn if you analyze what I write. After this chapter, you leave the tutorial and once again you control the takeaway, like your choice of actions.

Note before you say I could not survive without my parents. You are probably right, this is a different world, and I believe I did trade off interaction with people for harder classes, not saying I am not friendly but just a different type of person assuming you get my drift. As I already mentioned, the primary reason I am writing this is not for money because there will always be more of it, all I need to do is drop my hand in the bucket and pull some more out. A tool would be nice, but I cannot afford that, and those that can already have more than they know what to do with. This book will also double as a guide for my life and my future businesses. So no, I am not serving you a half baked product but for many, half baked is the most will they've ever had, so to actually taste it, and truly taste it, opens a whole new world. But if you did not figure it out yet I will be using my advice, which is what I believe to be the highest standard of advice and the proof of quality seal.

This relates to our own hypocrisy because we can be very quick to provide information, but when it is time to use it, excuses are made. But, just like everyone else, I do have financial goals, and I do wish this becomes "successful" and allows me to generate authority so all my hard work on this could be rewarded relatively quickly even though that would be inefficient, anyone who has won the lotto will tell you that. The greatest amount of taxes are taken with the biggest chunks of reward, and time is its own punishment or reward, it all depends on how the bottle is spun. Still, I have a feeling it is not going to happen this way and I am going to need to struggle a bit and make some sacrifices to get what I want. The process of going forth with this book is not going to be comfortable, and no matter what any publisher tells me I will keep my personality, and that includes this part because it is necessary, there is no reason to blur my thoughts because they appear useless, I do not know what can help, but I know what I would look for.

I recently fell back on my daily writing for a week, and there was not a valid reason for that to happen. It was not because I did not have any ideas, but instead, I did not want to put the work in at the time. There is no perfect time to do work, but you have to make it enjoyable, and that was something I forgot during this week. I am fun, and so is my personality as you have read, so I normally use my inside voice and edit. I get to make fun of my mistakes and laugh at some of the comments I make and treat it like a game so I can collect on the biological benefits of "winning" said game. But now I am taking accountability for my variance in choices as of late, and I want to use this to generate motivation to never stop again. Since motivation is not something that comes and goes with the wind, but rather happens after those five minutes of doing an activity. Which is why all it takes is five minutes to not stop the task at hand. As they say, everyone wants to lose twenty pounds, but is it worth it? So in my case, with this book, it is, and I am proud of that, yet I need to show it rather than say it. Anyone can say almost anything in most countries, but turning those thoughts into words then into action is an entirely different plane than the previous.

When you play the game of life make sure when you challenge others to share the rules in which you play, a game without limits is just a sandbox, due to the limits of rules is what creates the challenge itself. Working within confines is great and all but if your opponent does not recognize those confines, that could lead to issues. The moral responsibilities you set for yourself that seem like common sense, even though they are not, you need to communicate for them to be understood and recognized. As much as the rules need to be set, so does winning or total victory; what I mean is to define the terms. A real-life form of this entire paragraph is summed up into one word, contracts. But when you look at contracts you probably think of something shady or the lack of one's ability to generate unintended consequences but they are a part of life as well as the courtroom. Think about concepts and see if they apply and maybe if you get good enough at finding them, you can start to create them in your personal time to get better at it for your professional life.

Satisfaction

I want...
I want...
I need fun here,
Now there,
From one amusement park to another,
Riding,
Chasing,
Riding,
I want...
I lust...
I crave...
I need...
From a particle to a pebble into a rock growing to a boulder,
I want more;

Everyone one else has it,
I need more;
No one does not have it.

Everyone does them,
Without me,
So I say no,
I was a majority until I made myself a minority,
My steps lead to where I walk,
Try to catch up and keep up,
Those holidays,
Those fun times,
You can go if you want and keep craving more.

I put an end to that noise,
Silence is my new best friend,
My fuel is mine,
And I am the gas station,
Everyone can try to change the price,
But they are not me.

We are all different in many ways, but we are not even one in a million or billion, scientists claim we are around one in four trillion. By that logic, if your parents had more than four trillion kids there would be a duplicate, biologically. No matter, it is impossible to make two people have the same memory. Even if a duplicate person were to arise, you presumably would not notice if someone was a duplicate due to the slight changes in their perspective experiences, differentiating one person's memory from another, and due to things such as the butterfly effect. Since it is currently impossible to give two people the same time and attention, they cannot be perfect copies. Yet perfection is something we are taught to strive for from a young age, but is it a reasonable goal; no. Even with our knowledge of this, it does not stop our society from trying to make things perfect from auto-correcting grammar, thinking in theoretical situations, and using a logic that only stands in a utopia. A more straightforward way to put this is if you add anything to zero. Perfection is zero, and everything that affects it is a positive number that must add to it. Meaning that the moment anything is added to "perfect," even the circumstance will make it "imperfect." Note, there is no way to get a negative number, and the more flawed something is, the larger the number that gets added to it. Still, as long as you have even one slight mistake, it is not perfect, thus making perfection exponentially harder to obtain the more significant the system.

You will never be able to watch another oddly satisfying video without thinking of it from a biological standpoint. But oddly satisfying things are only that way because they are so perfect and it is at a level that it feels nice because we would never be able to achieve it ourselves; without machines or other such aids. The crazy thing about the mind, we like symmetrical faces as it is just how our ancestors used to judge health. But if we had a perfectly symmetrical face or person, which is impossible, we would be disgusted because it is too perfect-our brain then tells us that they are not typical/human. It's interesting how our brain already has a mechanism with the concept "too good to be true," in a sense. Yet we all still fall for scams that promise too many rewards for not enough work. There is a historical reason why we crave perfection in most things, and that is due to its appearance of survivability. What I mean by this is that by nature, we are expected to reproduce. Everything else is based on society, such as the wishful hope to struggle less, which was introduced in the form of nurture and not nature. All we needed was for them to survive, and to do that, we needed the best mate and the best food available. The best food was generally the brightest and most prominent, and that was considered the perfect fruit; it would not have any marks or lopsidedness. But often we would have to settle for something second-rate because we would either sacrifice our food or something would have found it before us and for us, it was okay to let the other animals or people have it. But the reason that we would give our food up to the leaders is a topic for later and a problem for the business world.

For the moment it is just about the same story, we want the best, but we take what we can get due to the fact that having kids - procreating - is better than not having any at all. And we get so fulfilled with completing the goals, we begin to look at ideal mates as goals needed to be completed, and every time one does get completed, it releases dopamine, which gives us a chemical sense of enjoyment, so we repeat it. So I challenge you to create a goal that is not based on competition but rather cooperation and complete it, for a change. Most goals in our society are looked at as competition but if you look on a broader scope you will realize it is inefficient cooperation, which is what we call competition. Do not get me wrong, there is a time and place for each, but perhaps a change in mindset can be enough. We got here through cooperation but when will the sights of competition be locked on something other than trivial instances based on ourselves. As society got more complex it evolved to where we would make our own homes, people would try to make them as big as they could as a symbol of meaningless achievement, although back then it showed value. But a house does not bring satisfaction, only the competition and the fact that you "won" even though there will always be bigger houses if you just look farther. Let's say you spent instead that time working on your own house to help build someone else's, satisfaction could last a lifetime.

The rhythm to a beat, if consistent for long enough, your subconscious will sync it to your heartbeat to it without you even noticing. One of our five senses is the ability to hear, used for survival, yet music has twisted it to be used to build people up rather than create paranoia as the dive-bombing sounds from world war one. Each person has a slightly different reality of a sound and taste leading to their being no perfect song except one that adapts itself to you. Your immediate taste in music can drastically change based on your mindset or headspace alone, not to mention by the people around you. To create the "perfect song," it would either have to be physically changing or it'll have to be "flexible." The inherent benefits of most music are that it increases the amount of oxytocin in your brain, which is your body's bonding chemical. Not only that but most people prefer the music to match their moods to improve it and that works in all states, including sadness and anger, to make oneself more pleasant.

Music is also most widely used for morale boost or happiness as most call it. But this music on chemical levels does more than just oxytocin; it releases a slew of chemicals that would take a page and a half to list all of them out. But this enjoyment that comes from music is generally associated with people, either the ones performing it or the ones that you are with but rarely with the actual people that wrote the script and created the tempo. Most do not realize the work that goes into a just a four-minute song from the pace to the snare, to the lyrics making it a near-impossible one-person job. That is for it to be "successful" as anyone can make a song but a good one is a challenge, but as technology evolves it is getting easier to do it all alone, compared to eras before the twenty-first century. Those who perform it are only part of the process but generally the final part, and if you just took the parts of the song and cross-referenced it with others it would either be bland at best or feel like another entirely. Especially with the sheer amount of music available to people, some of it has to be recycled from somewhere since there is no clean slate to mold from, because music is everywhere, from the songs we jam out to, to the background music we do not even acknowledge.

I am going to teach you how to hack your brain for productivity; I promise these are all legal. So for those of you that are in school and need to study here is the more efficient way to do it. The first thing is you need to find a spot, it can be anywhere, but it cannot be in a place that you currently use. So yes I am asking you to find the local abandoned section of your house, as you do. So I just talked with some of my friends about this and not everyone has an extra wing of their house that is not being used. Good news! You do not need that much space, it can be the corner of the floor that you are not using for anything, maybe about a yard squared and preferably uncomfortable. The reason it cannot be any space that you are currently using for any other task is that your brain is only so intelligent. So when you use a space for more than one thing, your mind does not know which one you are supposed to be doing at that point in time so it will resort to what item is most associated with that space, which is what you do most often in many cases. But every time you go into this unique space, your brain will already be thinking about that space whether you are consciously thinking about it or your subconscious is doing the work for you.

That is the same reason why using your phone in bed can be a bad idea, if your brain begins to think of the bed as phone time you will create your insomnia which would take some time to break and maybe a couple of hits of Nyquil later. That priming, although it might not be appreciated, does have a compounding effect. But if it were graphed the amount of time you are on your phone vs the amount of time you are sleeping, it can lead to some shocking results. For anyone trying to get over this, starving yourself is not the option, that will be painful. But you should slowly lower the phone usage in bed by about five minutes per night till you get your desired schedule. Since your phone can make your brain produce the same chemicals as certain drugs and from studying babies from "crack" addicts you can tell that removing is not the answer, they will die that way. Such as life, we are all constantly changing slowly, but if you look at where we were versus where we are you can see you are different. If you just woke up one day and see you've changed, that would mess with everyone you know with them thinking something happened because big shifts do not happen overnight and your brain knows that. Realistic example time: Bob uses his phone in bed about once a week for about five hours and complains he is bored while falling asleep, so he uses his phone to help him. That one time per week is continually setting him back never to get his brain to break the habit and understand that the bed is for sleeping and not Wikipedia diving. On the other hand, we have Jeffery, who also uses his phone in bed about every day for one hour each session, and he also complains about sleeping. He has the same problem with just about the same intensity because even though it is spread out over time rather than one big session, it adds up to the same amount of sleep loss so it is still the same amount of sleep loss.

The second step to study better is to have all your needs met already, so get yourself a snack, some water, and use the bathroom. Make sure every possible excuse is made and covered; your reasons are subjective. Just make use to identify them and find a way to eliminate them, beforehand. The third step is to tell yourself you only have to do it for ten minutes, ten minutes of full study time so I recommend buying a timer that vibrates but keep it far enough away that you need to listen to hear it and make sure you cannot see how much time you truly have left. I also recommend that you have your phone turned off entirely to stop the temptation or if you want to use your phone as a timer for whatever reason, go into settings and limit what apps you can access for those ten minutes of study time and set up a password to change those restraints. When I say set up a password, I mean give your phone to a friend or family member and let them create the password and make sure they remember it. Because your phone will let you hit "one more minute" a mere infinite number of times.

I do have a reason for why I said ten minutes rather than five, which is what everyone else goes with. That is due to the amount of information you are being bombarded with on a day to day basis.

Since there is so much information we "process" in one day, whether it be from school or a YouTube video about Tesla it is still some form of learning, no matter where it is from. So taking whatever you need to study and doing it for ten minutes means you will have enough time to reflect and process if you happen to let your thoughts get the best of you. Compared to it just being a short punishment, the time adds purpose. For everyone out there that does not need to study, I want you to test it for yourself, take ten minutes out of your jammed packed life, meditate on your day or week for ten minutes uninterrupted and watch the difference. You will most likely finish and be bored then transition into creative thought. But after those ten minutes, you will also have made enough of a commitment not to give up if you happen to need more time or you might even say to yourself, "look at what I have done in ten minutes let me just finish this in five more, and I'll be done." At least in my high school, when studying is brought up, it is like a competition for who wastes the most amount of time researching, almost like an auction. "I study for one hour a day." "Only that much, I do two." "I wish I had it that easy; I have to do three." It just keeps building up as I mentally shake my head because there is exponential decay when studying. The maximum amount of time you should study per day is minutes compared to hours. You are not learning but refreshing so treat it like that. Remember time is the limiting factor in life, generally and with that, you should treat it as valuable as it truly is and prioritize your study time. If you are getting a solid A in math there is no need to waste your time on it if it can be helped. For those who are not familiar with exponential decay, it is when the more you do something, the less helpful it becomes as compared to the previous time by losing efficiency.

Believe it or not, but you can choose whether you want to learn or not. Many say "why would I not learn something? You never know when it may come in handy in the future," and that is excellent logic. As I already said, it is way easier to say something, and it is an entirely different game to do it. We envy people like us, that are better than us at something, and choose that path of envy over the road of learning and growth. Sure, competition is high, but every product in a market does something better or worse than someone else, and people can learn from it, but what they would do if that product found success; to copy it. That thinking is based on the past, compared to thinking about the elements they got right and adding it to your already finished product. In essence, it is the difference between quoting and paraphrasing in writing. With quoting, it is someone else's words that you need to fit into your work and ultimately give credit and, in some instances, some of the profits. While on the other hand, paraphrasing is taking the source and putting a spin on it to accommodate your product. Though in a perfect world the second one seems like the better one, something I purposefully did not throw out was the cost of paraphrasing because if we bring this back to cooking. It takes a lot more effort to make something from scratch compared to using someone else's recipe but when you are cooking and you see an ingredient you do not like in their recipe you substitute it to better fit the product which is the taste. But the cost to paraphrase is not nearly as high as being the first to create it since in most cases you will need to fund the research not to mention testing and dealing with the regulations our society has even though it is there for customer safety, it can be a pain. Then the cost of actually putting it into production and the bugs that arise because of that, but the benefit to being the first is that you most likely will have the superior product, and you will have more marketing mumbo jumbo or an advertised item that no other competitor has.

Rather than speaking in formula format (X and Y) I will use a real-world example of being the first, Tesla the car company owned by Elon Musk, he saw a vision that no one else did and that was to make a fast electric car that anyone could afford and with superior quality. In contrast, the company did not make a profit for a while, but long story short; they finally did enough battery research to make them cheap enough and efficient enough not to burn a hole through the consumer's pocket or lifespan and for many eliminated "range anxiety." Now you are saying that is great and all but how does this get incorporated and to what, I say patience is a virtue and the sooner you accept that the more enjoyable life will be and the better your judgment will become. But back to what I was talking about before that moment of wisdom. Now (when written), most if not all car dealerships are trying to make electric cars because that new market is now "big enough" but that was not there before Tesla came and blew it open. So everyone is chasing Tesla. It is not fair to say competing, at least in that space. They are years ahead of their competitors because they were the first that stuck it in and rode it out to make profits. Some international car brands have been making electric cars for quite a while, such as the Nissan with their Leaf and Chevrolet with their Volt. Can we just talk about that name for a second?

"Hey, what do you drive?"

"I drive a Volt."

"Well, I guess I now drive a Watt."

"A what?"

"I thought we were both talking about fictional cars."

Now that that's settled we can now resort to our regularly scheduled broadcast. But they never dedicated their resources, according to the balance sheets they did but it was relatively low funding, it was nothing compared to Tesla. They just wanted to have a foot in the door and be able to say they had one but never cared for it even though they could have had a bigger budget than Tesla and researched it faster. Kind of like those terrible parents who had a kid just to have one but either does not have the means or the love for one. Still, they wanted to pocket the profits rather than reinvest, so when that choice backfires what happens is everyone scrambles and points fingers in a circle. Suddenly when they take Tesla seriously all these electric models and concept cars start popping up, with customers receiving them as short as two years out and a max of four because they want to have a chance at slowing Tesla down by using their powerful brand image that the customer supports and using it against them. But the money placed in marketing could be used for research and to help deliver a higher quality product, I do not know the cost for the marketing of their new electric cars, but I am sure it is not cheap and could impact other areas. Something that not many realize is that Tesla does not market its products on a commercial or over the radio, and that is due to the product being so far ahead; anyone that brought it will tell friends and family to get one because of its performance. Hence, there is less of a need, especially since their name is now out there with their stock being I don't even know how high. If you have a vision, others will want to join you, and they will find you rather than outsourcing.

We find money satisfying because it should solve all of our problems, yet there is no one solution to all of our questions; with money, it brings its unforeseen ones. You think your life will be better if you just made some more money. You think it could make all of your problems disappear, if only you made more money. Sure, a paid-off house is beautiful, and it reliefs pressure, but all that extra time will need to be filled. Free time is only good because there is a limit to it, so it has value based on scarcity. But when every moment is free time you lose yourself, especially if you do not have good hobbies since we are beings that need a purpose in a meaningless world. So we strive for something that we chase just to give it away because that is how others did it. Your world changes when you make that choice to decline extra money for a different job based on happiness. The power you get and feel from knowing that the money is not worth the cost of your sanity because in a world with no meaning, the perception of it is your only value till your vacation on Earth eventually disappears; or your suffering. As it is what you make of it, not what is given to you, get what you want because of you, as you are the only person you can feel, there is no point in making others "happy." Now not everyone will agree on this but we only make others happy because it will make us happy later in life, a basic investment, make a friend not be lonely, give a gift to a coworker only because you know they will return the favor. Now, let's say that you get enough money to live your life as a permanent vacation. It will be so annoying because you desensitize yourself to the value of vacation, and others will look and think she/he is so lucky to have a wealthy family, I would never be able to do that. Or, "Look, another rich kid decides it is too much when the going starts to get rough, shame he had such thin skin." Our problems are relative but that does not make them any less real, just like happiness, so you have no right to judge anyone else on theirs because if you were them you would do the same thing. If you had the same genetic makeup, same experience, and memories, you would do the same thing because you would be them and not you. Copying text from Word to Google Docs does not change the meaning.

The people we look up to, the heroes we look at all had a sense for delayed gratification and that is what got them where they are. George Washington went to a fort as a basic soldier to convince France to give the land to the British, and he failed. Tesla was founded in 2003, and it took at least ten years to become known and much longer for success. J.K. Rowling had to write under a pen name and post articles in the news; then Harry Potter came along. The satisfying thing for these people is the delay, almost as if they knew it would take hard work and time to complete. That is what builds the satisfaction they get. Going back to Newton's third law, energy equals energy out; if you got it instantly, the rewards would be close to nothing because there was not enough work built into it.

Think of it as shopping, if as soon as you wanted something, it would arrive at your door; it is way less exciting then if it builds over days or months because of shipping or money. You know the value of the object that you worked for, so when you get it, that work comes back as happiness. If it just appeared, then you would be desensitizing yourself to the work that others put in to get that same thing and wonder why it is not enough. I have all of what they have, and even more, why are they so happy you say to yourself. Then one day, you decide to ask how they are so excited, and they tell you we have just enough to get by. Because of that, we always need to have a conversation on what we are going to have for dinner based on money, and because of the lack of smartphones, we all have to talk and enjoy each other's company. The only way to find out what we have is to ask someone that does not have it. Some people do and do not have what you do, so use it to make you happy. For the good of a gift, not for bragging rights or to create jealousy as those you think care do not, and if they do, it is only temporary.

Time makes you wonder if you truly want something or if it is the heat of the moment or the peer pressure. So I thought about this and reflected on my life, and I can see all these rich kids at my school that drive these relatively expensive cars and thought I would like a new car. Then I thought, do I want to be the person that does not care about my phone knowing it will be replaced in a moment's notice? Do I want to be the one with a sports car even though I cannot drive a manual? Do I want to choose to be oblivious to the world around me? So I asked myself if a car was really what I wanted because I had the chance to get my license for about six months, yet I decided not to and so I asked myself again if this was what I wanted. Why did I not just do it already? That gave my answer; it was not the car I wanted, but then a

YouTube video came up with a motorcycle vlogger, and that was what I wanted. I knew it, but it was different because I knew what desire felt like, and this was not it. This was me, and this was my goal and choice after telling people what I want. I hear it is a death trap or, "If you decide to get it, it might as well be your mid-life crisis." I know what they mean, and I accept the risk of never walking off my bike, I want to ride, I choose to watch fatal crashes to learn from them and see how it happens. I know the risk, but it is one I chose and not one that was assigned. The car still had a purpose even though it was not for me; it showed me what I wanted. Just like how high school dating shows you what love is not (cannot confirm), that was my car. Something to compare my future choices to because I know what it is not, but here's the thing. There can be a lot of, "That is not for me moments as long as one, just one is the right fit. You can try a million keys that do not work, but each was still worth trying.

Motivation

Rising to fall,
Climbing to fall,
Trying to go up only just to fall back...
Down,
I was told to climb, but my coffin has no bias.

My mountain is mine, others are similar but
never the same,
My peak is a choice,
Not a religion,
This climb is not done alone but with others,
Giving their experience.

These shoes of mine are mine,
People try to claim it,

At the end of the day,
Whose feet are they on,
Mine.

I am still standing,
Tall yet short,
I will reach higher than everyone,
My mountain is the tallest out of all,
Your choice to be sharp will just make me taller,
The tallest people are the old robbers.
Let me grow,
Not by genetics,
But by skill and work ethic.

The countdown is the worst part of anything; the start is the most natural part. Most people only get to the preparation, then quit and believe they started. But if we are honest, most people are not willing to work eighty plus hour work weeks and struggle for years. The people that share the conflict, are the same people that can share their success and not the other way around. Those that come after your success want your success, not you.

I had a conversation with my mom while taking down the Christmas tree. She said firmly, "Just push those ornaments to me; they are cheap." Which is true compared to her Tinkerbell ornaments. However, I was gentle, so I retaliated with, "No matter the price, that does not change the fact that they are still an ornament and still hold sentimental value, and if you treat objects based on their worth then you are treating them wrong. The same goes for people, so remember a few days ago when you said next time someone does not say thank you for holding the door, to slam it on them." She muttered, "Yes." I retorted, "If you keep judging based on value, it's always going to be based on someone else's metric, and not your own. Like how you can exist but never truly live, now do you see why I cannot push the ornaments towards you." She stated, "I suppose."

The monetary value that things have is set by someone else whether you value the item for a lot or a little is your opinion but it is your choice whether you buy the item or not. However, if you treat something differently, just based on the value, your priorities can change quickly. If an old item you had suddenly gained value - it did not exist in your mind till it became valuable - but you didn't even keep it in saleable quality, and now you are desperately trying, nothing can wipe off all those years of negligence. But if you treated all your items based on your price tag then it would not matter the actual value of the object because you would have been happy with the choice you made. Nothing can truly take away the pain of the past, no matter the money or time spent, it still leaves a scar and it is one that you will need to embrace and move forward with.

It is about time I start to move on with my life from video games and laziness to positive habits and being responsible as a fully grown adult at sixteen. I already took it upon myself to start working out, and for the most part, I do it over ninety percent of the time; but, I need to get that to a hundred, there should be no reason, no excuse, I give myself not to do what I set out to. So I have to start walking on my two feet and all it starts with proper management of my time. I never had to study or focus for school or anything before this point, but if I had known I could do better, but I accepted what I got and decided not to push further, I chose to settle. I always used others as measurements, but those people are not me, they do not possess my skills, experiences, or intelligence. I wanted to start a business before I finish high school, but I always thought the idea was going to hit me until I realized nothing is going to change if I do not change anything myself. So I now have three business ideas with one of them already getting shot down before I had the chance to attempt it. With me proposing the other two throughout the month. But what I mean by getting my life back on track is to be a bit more normal, maybe if everyone does not decide for me I could get a girlfriend. Also start my journey into doing competitive shooting as well as accurately studying for upcoming tests or events to prepare for my future, but one thing I will not do is stress over those events. I am going to cut the things that hold me down, from my goals and rise to be the person that I am going to become. I will and am going to refine my writing allowing it to be a valuable asset in the future and potentially short-term cash to reinvest in myself to get better at what I need to. Over this year, I will improve my cooking skills to eventually make well over the majority of the meals for my parents and me in preparation for my future. I hope you got all those messages from that chunk and I hope you wrote them down because you will probably forget.

In our society, too many people can reject or disassemble you or your ideas yet, truth be told; most of the time, it is because they are projecting their failed dream upon you. Please do not get me wrong people want you to achieve goals but never more than their own. As if it is a race to make the most money or as if somehow we are running out of money, that mindset does not generate any positive feelings on a communal level and in most cases leads to failure, there is always more money you can get but it happens when you put the work in. Sure, it can help drive the person in question, but on a bigger scale, then that person will create a terrible atmosphere, even though a lot of us have that mindset. We want the best for everyone but never better than us, and sure it can be painted as selfish, but it is human nature to want the best for oneself then everyone else behind us. We are the ones that want our kids to be the best and not those that are not our flesh and blood.

When this conflict sets in, you try and justify reasons why they should not have gotten that promotion or why they should not have gotten that house, car, or job. Because we think that either they do not deserve it or that they are inferior to us in some overly minute way and use it to once again justify that it was luck and nothing more. These reasons are to prove to yourself that you are worthy but if you genuinely were, wouldn't you be in that position. There is always a reason why someone is somewhere and it generally is more than just luck. Most people see success and say it happened by chance, but luck equals "your position" times "immediate skill" equals "outcome" but others, and you determine if that outcome was favorable or not. Two people define success and failure, and sometimes they agree, but most times, they do not, and those two people are you and everyone around you. The only thing that should matter to you is your standards because it does not matter what anyone else does as long as you keep growing. Pro-tip for life, if you challenge yourself by about four percent higher than your current knowledge level you will learn much quicker than any other difficulty but that being said you do still need to incorporate other factors that improve learning to get the best results.

If you recognize something that everyone else does not, go with it and see where it leads, you could be right and/or you could learn why you were wrong, there are enough people that conform blindly. But when this opportunity is recognized do not let it get to your pride, you are not fast, everyone else is slower than you. That statement in itself should hold a lot of value and not be a cup half full or half empty story. The mindset that you choose will be where you end up. There are exceptions but if you believe to your core that you have worked hard enough, know enough, and struggled enough you will hit that goal. After all, if you are aiming where I am and that is the top we do not stop at good enough or at too much work. That is where we get up and start, every day is a new opportunity to push yourself past yesterday, MOVE! Do not wait for people to tell you when to do something do it NOW! The pain you feel now will be the same tomorrow if you do not do something, the more pain the more gain; no one that has made it to the top has taken it easy or will take a break.

These are just generalizations but overall the easy path was not a path but a road with a car, as you see the signs of your dreams and goals. Next right to Dreamland, where all is gotten for nothing. When it finally clicks, that the last four right-turns mean you are in the same place and you end up being too old to walk the bare footpath. There is no road to success but an ever-changing maze, no cheating, no following. Different for everyone but allows for the same people to make it to the end.

It goes a lot like this riddle: You want to get into the club but this bouncer requires a code so you watch as others go in. You hear the bouncer say, "Can." The lady says, "Three." He lets her in, the next man comes up and the bouncer says, "Dome." He says, "Four" and enters. So now you think you got it, so you walk up, and he says, "Kite." And you respond proudly with the incorrect number, "Five." But there are two other ways in which the answer to the bouncer can be calculated, one being the number of characters which would have made the answer four and another with the answer being number in the alphabet in which that first letter corresponds to making it eleven. It appears ever-changing, yet all those that get through will get through every time. Now, in this case, it was just finding the pattern executing a different story, but if you make it past the first step, you are infinitely more likely to continue.

Sure there are similarities, but just because you have those qualities does not inherently make you successful, we would have more successful people if so. Fun fact, future-proofing is generally the wrong way in the eyes of capitalism, most people see through that lens too but long term future-proofing is worth it if you can wait and make that sacrifice of money or happiness. The time without it counts as pain and it almost works like a compounding interest rate the longer it is in there the better rewards. What excuse could you give yourself to take a break? Turns out your brain makes a lot of them on a day to day basis causing your eight-hour workday to suddenly turn to a seven-hour one. We give ourselves breaks all the time and even though they are needed, we give ourselves way too many. Breaks are just an excuse to make progress.

When exercising some say the most gains happen right before failure, specifically the last five reps (repetitions) before failure. Most times we do not go till failure because we are afraid of it so we take a five-minute break and do it then and sure enough we get to the same point and give ourselves another. To get the best results, we need to reach failure. It shows us our progress and creates our goals, it teaches us what we need to improve or what gives upon us.

On the calendar, the only reason we get weekends and breaks for holidays is for the economy. Think about it, Black Friday was labeled that because that is when shops and restaurants went into the black. For people that are not aware of what black means it is when a business turns a profit so originally in debt/expenses was written in red ink and profit/revenue was written in black ink for two reasons one to make it easier to read and two to prevent manipulation numbers (My reasoning). Though the year for most businesses is different than our calendar years for pretty obvious reasons. There probably are many reasons for this but from my seat, after Christmas, some of the things we do not use are instead, returned and rather than a business having to worry about that influx of loss at the beginning of the year they choose a less volatile time to do it.

We climb out of bed, we walk on the paved road, for what? In the end, there is no reason for life or death, all will be forgotten and all would have happened. I know this is counterintuitive but nothing matters in the grand scheme and if you do not think so look on a bigger scale. So what you find is the cure to cancer, so what you sacrifice is yourself, congratulations you will be forgotten and you will not impact the "grand plan." But the thing that does matter is what you feel because in a world where nothing matters, you do. You have to enjoy yourself or at the very least have the opportunity to, we are not here just to reproduce but to enjoy ourselves as that is the only thing truly real, but only real to us. This feeling may pass very soon or stay for a while, but for common courtesy, there is no reason to be a statistic no matter the difficulty. I have known great statistics, but if life is here for us to enjoy why end it even if it is pointless to think about the kids. The people you have illuminated their days to bearable levels, the future you could have, the boss you like to work for. It seems so far but you need to take that first step whether it is going back to school or searching for a new job. Not all of your life will go your way but making the best of it is your full-time job and you have a right to help others.

I can only speak for myself here. Like many things, it is the foundation that determines when the building falls; not the size, color, or shape. Set a goal to reach and hone in on it. It can be as simple or as insane as you like but what matters is that every day you work towards it because you will forget and you will get lazy if you do not interact with the project daily. The minimum you can do for a project is to think about it, if it does not come to mind then you might want to increase its priority. My current and most important goals rely on me and not a number or static. They need to be done by me and sure others can help but they cannot do it for me. Remember that your life is not a train wreck or a company that needs to supply a number, go at your own pace but with every failure learn something and make sure your mentor is truly a mentor and not a shadow of their knowledge. Analyze your teacher to make sure they are masters of their atmosphere, if they are not you might be wasting your time. You came to learn and not get automatically passed. This does go towards making sure you want their knowledge to grow and improve your ideas and not to become their ideas. I will say, again, make sure you do it for you, and not because you want to be them, you can try but you will fail.

I had to learn that lesson and I realized it with something I decided to stay with, even though it was tough. That was motorcycling, they said it was hard and almost impossible to fail according to the internet so I went in and failed the practical section but I stayed to get the written part out of the way. Yes, I was annoyed and disappointed at first, it was the only thing I cared about that I failed. So yeah, everything came through my mind. "Maybe it is not for me. I wasn't that interested in it. I might have been destined to fail this like maybe I was set up to get extra money out of me." As I sat there and watched the instructors I noticed that they never really had to get on the same page, they were always there, so that piqued my interest. So rather than going on my phone, I decided to pay more attention. Then I noticed that they moved certain people from the inner circle to the outer circle and I did wonder why, were they bored? I noticed that as they moved some of them, it made the entire process more efficient, they were watching the students and judging their skill and moving them accordingly on the fly. To many, that was just a choice they made and nothing more but that is when I knew it was their exam I had to pass. I could not go anywhere else, they have seen it all and have worked with it all, that changed the question in my mind from if I am going to pass this to when am I going to pass. Now for those of you that are not familiar with the process of getting *legal* in the U.S., you- basically- need to take a two-day course and then you are *legal* and once you get your driver's license you can go for the motorcycle one. But in many cases, people learned on dirt bikes or just rode dirty till they got caught. So they show up to the class to use it as leverage to fight the ticket. So the class of eight people had all ages, it was not just high school students, it was not just guys and it was not just the inexperienced and I had to get that last part through my head.

You need to enjoy your hobbies now for the kid at the back saying I do not know my hobbies I ask them. What type or content of YouTube videos do you watch, and that content is a hobby you could be living out. But never stop something if you know you need to do it. Being lost is a part of the process, do not rush it, maybe time will light the path you need to take but do not expect it to just hit you. Go but do not go, Add but subtract, we all start and end in the same place we all need to eat and sleep but that does not take up your whole day. Find balance and like riding a bike you need to just get on and try to go and fall and fall some more. Get wiped out a couple of times, no one says you need to try for your entire day and no one says that it will not click instantly. Just get up, things will be a lot tougher than you think, and do you know how I know that? Because there are things tougher than me, you, you, you, and also you (points at different people); even movies make the main character have a conflict, if Hollywood realized this it must be beyond common knowledge.

But my goals are to write this book as a first, the second one is to have a killer six-pack and the third main goal I have is to get a motorcycle. Even though this is SAT (Scholastic Aptitude Test) week at school and this is a determining factor in what college you get into. It is a test that is monopolized by a nonprofit which profits, it is a test that is curved based on the relative difficulty to all others, it is the reason many lives are taken per year. It is on things you have never learned and probably never will, but it can be beaten by thinking outside the box, everyone buys the book and tries to learn the content and everyone knows or has their own test-taking strategies but what about learning the questions? If you do not understand the question you cannot get the answer accurately so if you were to cross-reference the wording of the question to the answer eventually there will be a pattern which will make taking the test faster and increase your scores. For this to work you need to create an A.I. that will take questions and answers as inputs, it will surmise the question and the answer in a compact form and write the percent chance of each answer type being the answer based on the question. Now, this would take a lot of manpower or SAT questions and answers, everything else is proper coding. Your score is like your GPA and it is the kid version of salary, you are judged upon it, the higher is better, someone has a higher whatever it may be, it changes. You cannot worry about your friends getting something before you because it is not a race for what place but if you finish. That is why my goals are not toward school which is vaguely useless in the United States.

But back to my goals, this book, every day I try to write at least a page slowly making progress and not allowing my habits of procrastination to take control because yes I do have a projected deadline but it is adjustable. I just have it so I can hold myself accountable but if it takes a week or even a month longer, that is okay. The same thing can be said for my second goal of getting ultra-fit. It is not because I want an easier time getting a girlfriend, although many might see it that way. But I have always been small and skinny so now I want to tone up and become strong for myself so that I may become the person people ask to open a jar. For this, I need to work out every day without fail because when I say not today, it becomes not tomorrow till it reaches never as you look back on your memories and wonder what happened. I am a believer in that there is never a bad investment in yourself. I also want a motorcycle not because I - totally - want to half my total lifespan, but rather because it provides me with way more smiles per mile than a car, and if you do not make the process fun it will feel like a long ride. I want it to be a journey that I want to commence and never end, and that is what I want to feel every time I leave. The freedom and the air swirling around me are just invigorating even though I may get the wind knocked out of me. I know the cost of what I am doing and I have no reason to be scared or worried, I trust myself and every driver I meet. I know that I may give up the chance to walk off my bike but I am not going to let that control me. Yes, there, of course, is some form of fear because without it you are reckless but I have made my choice and that is mine. Try to take it, I dare you.

Motivation is special in that you can read as many books or motivational videos as you like but the desire still needs to come from within. That inner dragon you had when you were a child needs to be released, that excitement from learning and improving the tiniest things needs to come back. You need to do it so when I ask fellow peers what they want to do I ask three questions. One, what do your parents want you to become? Two, what do you want to be? Three, if there was anything in the world you would want to do, what would it be? I want number one to know if number two is them or someone else is forcing them. Just like how it is easy to waste someone else's money you can easily do it with your life, especially when considering one of the top reasons people have children is to live out their failed dreams in the form of their kids. Most people call this living vicariously but I decided to not use the vocabulary word. Question two should be equal to question three. So when they give me a different answer I have to ask them why they are different. They are the same question just spoken in different semantics yet normally create different answers. When I say "want to be" it makes it sound like a more realistic approach like what is going to happen extrinsically and on the third question I say "anything in the world" and that makes people think outside the box to an end goal and a more creative answer. Ask yourself these questions and we will continue.

Now we need to get your mindset from question two all the way to question three and the first step in doing so is seeing yourself. You need to imagine what it is going to look like because when you can see it you can chase it. The second thing is that at the very least do one action to get you closer to where you need to go. If every day you do something related to the destination then you will become addicted to completing your goals. It also helps if you work on it every day there will be no procrastination or big amount of pressure because you are doing it over a reasonable period compared to the eleventh hour. The third thing is that you need to stay with it till your grave and even after. I say this because there were many authors in history where they wrote good quality "stuff" but they released it at an inconvenient time causing it to not get the appreciation it deserved until years later, and for some, even after they died. Step four, have that goal listed everywhere possible: the fridge, the door, the bathroom mirror. Everywhere that you go, to remind you of your goals, and have your brain constantly thinking about it so that you become addicted.

Those were the four steps for motivation, productivity, and the path to accomplishments but more on that will be discussed later on and as I remind you about it, it will become easier to remember. And just because I know people are going to forget what I said earlier, I will repeat myself. It needs to come from within, a goal that is yours and it has to be at the forefront of your mind. If it is just on the back burner like you think about it every once in a while, it is not a reasonable goal, to do something you need to focus on it. Most say unreasonable goals are only for those that are too big but it can also be for those that are too small and often that is the problem. Because when it is too small, it is when you finish it just to do another thing. To make the original goal function an example would be if your goal was to make an engine, now that you have it, you cannot do anything with it, you have no clue whether you wanted to see it or attach it to a transmission and eventually a car. Small goals will create a haze in your mind and can lead to the feeling of being lost although you are not; specificity matters. If your current goals tie into a higher goal then that should be your goal and have that task as a stepping stone. But once you have your goal you need to expand it, factor it, then simplify it. If you are not strong in math you - basically - treat it like a puzzle, you need to take it out of the box, which is *expansion*, then you need to find the edges and finally sort pieces based on color, and then and only then you can solve (If you follow this method, you could technically brute force it but take a page out of a hackers book and use efficient methods to do things rather than the simplest). A common effect that happens in strategy games is snowballing and it also happens in life, in both good and bad situations. When you are feeling good you are more likely to get into the state of flow which increases productivity and you are then impressed by your results which makes you feel even better like a theoretical permanent happy times. But if something happens, you get dumped - for example -, your inhibition lowers which means that you are more likely to make bad choices. Alcohol has the same effect but if it is generally more potent with a substance and especially with substance abuse. My recommendation for breaking down goals is to use a flowchart. I made mine digital so every time I use my phone or computer I see my progress and I cross off what I finish, to get some of the snowballing effects. Note that I said cross off and not remove, a lot like events that you can deal with but never remove them in their entirety. So try to make a flowchart to the best of your abilities of what you need to do and it can be broad as long as you know what you need to do because this is your goal, I like one to five words. Everything on that flow chart is a task that needs to be completed and every day you should cross an item off of it. Note that they are not goals, goal is a word I reserve for the end result because it makes your brain give you a bigger boost in dopamine because it is called something different and it has a significantly lower frequency. Keep in mind all the steps are just that, steps but when you look down from the mountains all those steps show themselves and how they have paved the way. The same notion can work with working out. After every workout you feel good for a short amount of time but when you one day decide to look in the mirror or have that girl check you out, it pays off. You remember the before and see the after, little do you know that the same logic can be applied to many facets of your life.

If you need to get passionate and driven quickly, head over to a sales department where people are paid on commission. The reason I say this is because society is based on money and your hard work equals the amount of money in your pocket. The work you produce has to be good quality so that it forces you to have a contagious drive to make the monetary mark they set for themselves, and afterwards if they were to be satisfied they would pay you by the hour. Anywhere, where there is no ceiling it is where you see people that do not settle. It tests their drive and commitment since they have no excuse other than themselves because most jobs have their salary or set amount range of income, real estate for the most part is purely commission and that is why most in the business have made tons of money. If you did not get what I was saying, this means that in real estate what you take home is based on how much you sell. Those that do not make an effort will quickly find out you can not just cruise on through this career, so it eliminates those that choose to not work hard. It is not easy or served on a silver platter but if you put that much work into it you will get the same returns one way or another. The universe is just like that but it will not be as evident as you want it to be. I believe it defines you when you have no cap in the same way you test a good person by not having anyone enforcing rules. They will naturally do their calling since no external factors are swaying their decision at least ones that we can eliminate.

There is no perfect day to start and there is no day to skip. If you let an excuse get in the way then there will be another, whether it is today or tomorrow it will happen. If you wait for that day to finally come to start something you will be six feet under. Waiting when nothing is stopping you is just wasting, nothing more, nothing less. But for those who want to get better at their craft, make every reason to do it more often, it could be volunteer work at the office or just some after school practice. You define the intensity but any chance you have to do it should be seen as opportunities that are meant to be taken not chosen. Just as you say no to that opportunity, others will say yes and that person might just end uping work above you because of that extra work. You chose that other activity over that "extra work", no reason to place blame, just accept it and move on, hopefully learning from that experience. That person that chose that "extra work" most likely missed out on something else in their life and you just wont witness it. Know that it was a choice and it did come with positive and negative outcomes that are relative, but ultimately everything is balanced. Just as there is matter there is the antimatter with the absence of one comes the absence of both.

Remember that just because you do not see something that does not mean that it is not there, just like how the oven does not look hot it does not mean it isn't. Oftentimes, we look and we can even look thoroughly but that does not mean we are looking in the right place. When I play strategy games with my friends I tell them to stop looking with their eyes but with their minds, because seeing something is halfway to believing. And when you see an acceptable solution you do not truly dig deep to see if it is correct, a lot like the "I got framed" card. But maybe that's not your issue, if self-esteem is your current struggle, I got you. Notice that they may make more money but you may have an unbreakable bond with your partner, do not make yourself seem better or worse because we are all equal but never equal; therefore, acknowledge they are on the same playing field as you. Though the same must be said for people that you believe are less than you, and you have no right to judge the choices they make because they are not yours and you do not know one hundred percent of their life. Overall thoughts can sometimes not be helped but make sure they do not affect your actions. But as for the deep, "equal but never equal" thing that will be for the next segment, after all, I need to make sure you still have a reason to read the following bits, hashtag marketing, that is right I did just type that, enjoy the cringe.

Pathfinder

Be the man that does what he has to.
S-suffer,
S-slowly,
Q-quietly all around me,
Just needing a pause,
To stop;
Smelling the roses along the way,
Living in a constant state...
But not reality.

Hold.
Look.
Fire.
That was your past;
This is your future,

No control Z,
Making the present just a past reality,
Look back to learn,
Look forward to seeing,
Today is a dream.

Caught in a bad dream,
With monsters in my head,
Screaming,
Wake up already;
It has to be morning,
Most already know...
The day is where the actual monsters hide,
How should the light purge the darkness or
does it mask it;
Creating the biggest masquerade party in
history,
The struggle between light and dark,
The fight between itself that will never start
or finish.
It is making everyone a casualty.

At some point or another, you will think
about kids and perhaps how many to have, but you
realize there never is a perfect amount and I am
going to show you later, to make a better point. But
for now, let's talk about choices, and how it is your
greatest freedom but never one you control. Now
that statement at face value must be a lie due to

the fact that you choose dinner because you say you want pasta and it happens, but there are third party factors involved in that decision in itself. Right now, as you probably know we are living in the age of influence, there is an ad everywhere you look as well as thousands upon thousands of brands all attempting to make a good impression on you to ultimately get your money.

I am not going to say it is morally wrong or anything, but nothing you choose to do is completely out of your free will. For example; when you were watching an ad on a cleaning product and they got the pasta on their shirt and removed it with a nice jingle you did not get the message of the ad. But you were not the target, it was your subconscious and it did get the message but every time it hears that jingle it reinforced the previous notions of the ad. Till one day you get the pasta on your shirt and are suddenly drawn to this product on the shelves. As you're in line, you have already justified that it is going to work with no actual evidence, you just feel confident for some reason so much so that you talk to someone in line about it and they too buy it. It does not matter if the product worked because it got two sales or at least one minimum.

The best targets for an attack are the ones no one expects, this goes for anything. In chess, many people think the queen and the rooks are by far more likely to get taken because of their sheer usefulness but if your opponent gets the knight out of the way everything else is just working with lines and that is way easier to process and therefore win but not many people think about that. They think about value and not efficiency. Even though you have one mind, that does not mean it is used that way, like partitioning drives. For the brands you support, think of a reason why, maybe it is the project for the community that they did and that's great and the opposition might have done more but they just did not use it to promote their brand image. Pay attention to the fact that biases are everywhere, and even though there is no avoiding them, you can at the very least realize them to challenge your beliefs. I find too many people have their minds made up on something and when asked why they do not say why they just state "because it is" even when you throw proper information at them. It is because beliefs are being challenged and today as open as we are about including everyone and not judging, that is very limited in the grand scheme, we need people to listen to both sides and choose or create your own middle ground so that it is based on your own thoughts and on your own reasons. Now what I mentioned did not include manipulation or misinformation being present, even though it probably is to some degree. To that I would honestly chalk it up to the law of large numbers because odds are both sides are going to have about the same amount of twisted facts and "too good to be true" results to the point where it could cancel out.

One of the main reasons why I decided to talk about dead set minds is because of my mom, I love her and everything but when her mind is made up about an idea it is hard to change it. So for fun, I decided to ask her what's the difference between *cooperation* and *collective cheating*, now she did not know the definition of *collective cheating* within this conversation but she did know what cheating meant and so I asked her about her thoughts on it, now if we pause. It is hard to argue when you do not even know the true values of the other side, but her response was not her thoughts but more so societies thoughts opinion of it and what those actions can look like if I were to get caught but I did not ask for that, I tried again and got almost the same lecture word for word and could not even attempt to justify my side before getting cut off. Now collective cheating is either you do 4 problems and I do the last four and we give them to each other or I do one assignment and you do the next one and so on. But you cooperate to fix a problem, my problem was not with the question but rather on the whole assignment or the class so we cooperated on the assignment and I did half as well as you or we cooperated on the class, I did half the work and so did you. So we were cooperating and we were also using a credit system and had trust that the other person would do their share and send it, and basic game theory made it stand. But overall they are the same and if I get caught I will make that argument because it is true, it is wrong because morally we are not doing what is assigned to us but in a company, it is technically the CEO's job to run the business yet they hire people but that's cheating because even though it is their job to do they are getting others to do it, and rather then trading work for work they are trading work for money and money is a physical form of work. I want to hear people's arguments that are against this because cheating is the exception to cooperation. I wish that rules were laws and not theories, now that's deep or should I say solid.

There is never a perfect number of brats to have and that in itself shows that there is no perfect decision they all have consequences, but it might be more appealing to you based on your values or lack of responsibility to the negative effects, but that does not mean it is perfect. People say to aim for win-win situations and I have to agree but if you look at the choice with a scope you will see that there is no such thing as win-win, it does have some sort of balance which is why I believe the first law of thermodynamics is not limited to everything but all-encompassing like a true should be. Although it would be naive to think this worked in all planes of existence I do think it deserves more credit then potentially a physics experiment.

Those little flies at the back of your head controlling you, judging you, are mainly there because you let them in and choose not to squash them, maybe for personal reasons or due to obliviousness. Identifying and eliminating them with accuracy can remove the obstacles in your life and allow you to follow priorities or goals set with greater motivation and less of a drain on one's day to day energy. If allowed to stay the effects can be similar to any lousy habit, most of the downsides are not seen until you go down the road, man life needs more road signs or like some bright lights on them, almost as if you can google seniors and you would be able to find the "favorable outcome" in like two minutes flat. But the effects of letting manipulative people into your life compound with the more you let then and one day you wake up and wonder "what happened to my life" a lot like the guy that went to the gym but the opposite, he looked and said, "I remember back then I had to work my butt off and now it is so simple and I look amazing, turns out the party life was the biggest mistake I did not make". The formula for the effects is the same and that formula is not a secret and it is definitely not related to genes or IQ (intelligent quotient). Who knows maybe an angel will fall from the sky and either give you some mortality motivation or the answer to your problem either way if that happens to you, I would bet you are crazier than everyone else.

These people have an onslaught of tactics that they use to control and manipulate people as it can be as simple as a day job for some people or more skilled ones unconsciously, and most have more weapons than actual victims. However, that being said victims are relatively long term commitments although most manipulators have at least twenty victims. Now putting that into perspective, let's say there is the same number of manipulators as there are sociopaths - even though in reality this number is high - but one point five percent of the population is the estimated numbers of a sociopath so doing some quick math one point five percent times twenty equals thirty which means at the true minimum thirty percent of the population has been a victim and some do not even realize it and yet we talk about more trivial issues that have a way higher chance of never happening to us in our lifetime. The process is not as simple as filling up gas although some might make it look that easy, it requires energy, but most times, it is pointless for a victim to counter these strategies based on the sheer number of weapons that can be used. It is easier to walk away before a connection is formed, but you will not realize it then, but once it is formed breaking it might leave you feeling guilty for your actions even though in the back of your mind you notice life getting easier without them and cannot seem to figure out why. Most times, the knife is stuck in so deep that you will bleed out if you pull it out, but once it is gone more of yourself can be there. That is one of the patterns with those types of people, it's that they would rather be in a lose-lose situation than a win-lose so their last-ditch effort is basically to take you down with them. So when you remove them, they make sure to play all the emotional cards just because they know that you will think about them in the future and every time that happens they win. Nothing is supposed to be comfortable, and they use that to their advantage since they know people like to avoid pain, for the most part. My advice for life, get used to being uncomfortable.

Jobs are like any other skill, requiring practice and active use to keep it nice and shiny. It is not a talent, and for the most part, it is a level playing field. The exciting part is when you run into someone else and see how they do it because there is no one way of doing something, there might be a better way but it is never old, that's just naive. But most likely they will do it differently, even if it is just slightly and that subtle difference could save you an insane amount of time in the long run. Either in a minor or significant way, but no matter what, a lifelong learner will always... learn, whether its a way to not do something or a way to do it or a way that works under certain circumstances. They will find a takeaway and somehow incorporate it, though this is not limited to one party, everyone involved has the opportunity to learn something. Everything has a foundation associated with it; you do not just start at the top; you build up to the top.

Things on a fundamental level all have a base and a separate higher level to where the societal standard is. Even in simple things such as language, we first started with crying then grunts, if you will, and you slowly start to string syllables along till you become your average American. It is explained a lot better with writing, so here it goes. You start with letters, then words, phrases, and sentences. This is the basic level at which you can function in society, and over ninety-five percent can manage this. A letter is a full sound and a word is a collection of letters that has a definition. A phrase would then be a finished image and a full sentence is a thought. Then it builds to paragraphs which are full of ideas to chapters which are complete items and so on. But there is an exponential decay on every level, so fewer and fewer people make it past the chapter level, which is about a research paper. This does not only apply to this area of expertise, but rather every area in which there are different levels of skills that can be measured.

The average person is a jack of all trades and that is not bad. However, our education should be more specialized in making people better at what they do so that time is not wasted on things that do not matter to them, such as American history, which is less than three hundred years old. Which I assume is vaguely useless for a physicist or engineer, but I could be wrong, what do I know, I am only sixteen. But at the same time, people do not know what they want to do, and that can be seen with the odds being that a person will change their major more than once instead of not change it at all, this happens when there are too many options to where we just go with something we never really wanted, which happens to be called *over-choice*, convenient. The reality is that life only starts past eighteen and I plan to crush it. We do parallel processing with computers but how come it does not happen with our heads, waiting is wasting, we already know what happens to our environment when we waste. I believe most, if not all, buildings do not stand with a damaged foundation, but some teachers do not teach and the year after they expect you to know things that the previous teacher did not teach causing the students to be lost and always a couple of steps behind the ones with a solid foundation, that "mastery" of past subjects. Buildings are made to survive all forms of weather yet our education system does not account for it, if they are teaching the next generation, what message are they sending, think in perfection or perhaps go from one to four, sometimes you gotta take a step back and look at the actual message, not just the one advertised as the loudest action is often the quietest.

A lot of people throw around the word *organization* whether it be for a group of something or for a system of finding things. But when people say I am not organized I ask them if they know my system because - apparently - there is only one way to be organized. And it is one that everyone can automatically know, which from my knowledge is impossible so I hand them a military technology, GPS tracking; it works so well. Upon entering my space, there should be no reason to impose an organization system, if it appears chaotic or messy ask me where something is and if I cannot find it easily then mention whatever organizational system you use. The point is that organizing is done by the user and just because "organized" people have a system that happens to be user-friendly does not make them the only ones that fall under this category. I call myself organized but my system is that I put items in places not by alphabetizing them or by its "friends" but by sorting them based on their usage. This method seems foreign to so many people that it amazes me, and this works surprisingly well when you get used to it; try it for a week. I take my future thanks and walk away.

But here is a little life hack that I found out whenever, without fail, you look for something, check the last place you looked. Some of you might not get it but what I mean by this is not to literally check the last place you would even thought it might have a good turnout. But when searching for an item you do not look for it after you found it thus making the last place you looked is where it always is. Even though this was just about the most useless life hack you have ever heard it is not far off from some of my whittier comments even though it is more helpful than "5-Minute Crafts." But back to the topic at hand, I know where the fair majority of my stuff is because of this system yet most see no "logical" rhyme or reason, easily. So they assume I put things wherever and that is what it is but even after I explain to some people they do not see the value of it. This is yet another situation where I would tell people to look with their minds and not their eyes but you can only do so much for people that have made their choice. So I let them ask me where vaguely common items would be and sure enough, I respond with about one hundred percent accuracy. I, personally, do not have time to waste on finding things and I know most of you do not either. To find the system that works best for you is the best since I already stated that but it creates some level of balance to find something easily. As you should know, everyone else does not matter unless you are married and in that case, you have to do whatever the wife says without fail, yet we are equal, just saying. As for the fine print, note those items that my friends asked me about above were commonly misplaced items but not just general commodities ones.

We all have attended and we all give it consciously or not. You can expand it but never have enough and skilled individuals can manipulate it either on a small scale or on a massive one. For a small scale attention whore, you can look at a pickpocket. Most of the time you see their face, and odds are they bump into you. When that happens your attention shifts from what you were focusing on before they bumped into you, but in that split second your wallet is gone and that is due to your sensory adaptation and lack of attention. For those not familiar with the term it is when you have something on you but you do not feel it because your body classified it as "background noise," until you focus on it. A prime example is your shirt. Think about it for a second, you now feel it, but before you knew it was on without feeling the fabric as you do now. Hopefully, you are reading this book with a shirt on, if not it also works with any piece of clothing or any item attached to you for an extended time. Just saying you are a very different type of person if you choose to read with nothing on, not judging, just saying. Back to the important information, when someone bumps into you I would hope that you expect them to in some way touch you so when it happens your attention is shifted to the person that you have now given a colorful name and a plan to never see them again. But you do not expect to feel something in your back pocket when you get bumped on the front so you do not feel it, perception is reality, you think they are clumsy so they are until you look for a wallet. For a larger scale attention grab, it was first used in the military and became a thing a little after guerrilla warfare came about. But it was the whole bait and attack mentality which most call an ambush or stakeout.

Now sure you just learned at least one thing so far, assuming all this information is relevant and that also assumes that I know something that is not common knowledge, I could just be extremely naive. But the actual points come down to the fact that if you choose to fully read this book and take it seriously, you will read it again as you reach new stages of your life and every time it will change that little bit making it almost like a fresh read with the same plot. The average person's retention rate when reading is around ten percent and if you are the type of person that is listening to this in your car it is closer to five percent and not to mention it is harmful to you and those around you based on that limited attention, but it is not as bad as texting. So you do you and I'm flattered but sacrificing yourself to get only five percent is what I call unnecessary risk. Just because you listened to it on the way to work and one day you do not hear a horn and... *glass shattering.* This can also be an argument that has two sides, as many do. Now it is time to go in-depth on each side. It is great for those who would not get the information otherwise because of their limitations. If we look on the other side, if you planned on reading it then it is pointless to listen to it but it does save time but then I ask are you trying to complete the book or learn from it. There is no point in saying to someone that you completed something because no one cares but what you took away from it can help you whether it is now or if it helps in the future. I cannot guarantee that it will help but I believe it will if I thought it was useless I would not have included it after all this is going to help me as I continue to age.

I repeat phrases a multitude of times and there is a reason for that, but no, it is not because I cannot think of anything else to say. I use it to prime your subconscious to have an idea of what the sentence is going to be about. As much as you might believe it is due to a lack of intellectual capacity; it has a good reason. Since you have two *attentions*, technically one that you are currently in control of and are aware of, and the other that works in the background and allows for the most depth and highest level of critical thinking even though it might overstep its boundaries and be slightly more magical. Most believe the only one that matters is the one at which you are actively aware of but if you only look at the surface you cannot appreciate the complexity. Think about a zipper, it seems so simple yet it took years to make one and most people take it for granted because it is small, cheap, and readily available but it is still a complex mechanism once you open it up or choose to reverse engineer it. Most believe they know how it works but if you ask them and know how it already works you might be able to teach them something new. I am going to give you homework, after and while you read this book go through and figure out what repetition is used to prime your brain to where I want it. The reason I want you to do this is that since you are interacting with the content of the book it allows for you to understand on a whole other level that you would most likely not come close to if you were just reading it.

That is part of the reason all sorts of things have brand names on them so one day when you need that object, you think of one that you have seen in the past and because it has a brand you instinctively look there first. And since many do not do their research on what they buy especially if it seems inconsequential then they go with what they are familiar with, generating easy sales for the company. That is why odd things have branding on them because when you need them, previous customers work for the brand, even with niche products like a power strip. Even though an item is just an item it becomes a brand if that company you are exposed to creates associative ties with you. If all you see is Hewlett-Packard (HP) computers at work, school, or wherever you think internally that this brand must be good because enough people use it, that all manner of second thoughts leaves your head. Compared to that new eBay seller that is selling what you want for an incredible price but because they have not gotten a review you question your decision and ultimately pay for credibility and that is how brands like Apple make so much money. When you buy from a brand you do not only pay for the item, you have to pay for the name brand, features with the company, and its image. When a brand is powerful it brings a message and a person to mind. Imagine if Apple was the only phone company that you knew, then you would have to spend the money since it appears like your only option, people do not like leaving their box so they have to come to them before their box closes. Appearances become reality to those that are okay with the surface.

When finding yourself, forget that you knew you and move towards the future. Holding on to things for too long can lead you to form a terrible habit or problems in relationships with broken/missing physical items. Whether it is that girlfriend that you still believe you have a shot with even after you broke up with or that broken television that you made many memories with; it is okay, your world will not end. Remember the times but let go of the past, put it back to when it was supposed to be. But on the opposite side of things do not just quit because they are too hard or because it will not look as good. In most cases you do not know what people look for, you may think you do but you probably do not.

A prime example is college and me, I still am slightly uncomfortable with sharing this but it must be said. In my high school life, I have always taken AP (Advanced Placement) classes and when they were not available I would succumb to honors classes. Even if they were not in my prime subjects such as freshman year when I took AP Biology. It was a hard class, to begin with, and it was made for Juniors to struggle in so I walked in and put equal effort into it and I got a D on my report card so I had two options: drop the class or stay. So I convinced myself that hey I might get better, that was only in the first quarter, or it could have been a fluke. Second-quarter rolls around I get another D and at this point, I knew I should have been studying but I have not done it for any other class so why this one, why does this get special treatment so I did not and long story short ended with a D but on the final exam every biology student on campus needs to take to graduate and end of course (EOC) exam, I get a high four out of five meaning that I was in the top fifteen-ish percent of Biology students; in the district, so it was not because I was incapable I very much was it is just the fact that I do not think the school should have let any freshmen into AP Biology and sure enough next year they did not so yes I blame the school but at the same time it is what made me a part of who I am so I cannot be too mad at it. In the end, my parents did not force me enough to get higher then what I ended up getting so I settled with my grade because it was good enough for me.

But what I could have easily done to remedy this was to make my guidance counselor drop the class and that is what most did and I saw those as quitters because for all they know that first test could have been a fluke and they would never have known because they dropped it. But here is my reason for why I take AP. It is because I do really want the credit or the look but rather the fact that

I might learn something there I may never have learned otherwise. So I could have dropped it but I did not because I did not take it for the grade and with that, it still haunts my marks and my guidance counselor said to me that it would be a good idea to retake it at a lower level and get that easy A. And as great as that sounds, I gave her four reasons why I wanted to choose to stay with it and why I will not retake it.

The first one being that if it was just a test yeah, okay I would have done it but that was too difficult even after summer I still have vaguely enough knowledge about all that organic stuff to retake an EOC to replace my grade, but once again that option was not possible. But the second relates to why I did not quit and I gave her a scenario which was, "You live in an apartment that has the lowest rent in the city and when you realize the cost of it you understand that you cannot pay for it so your choice is to become homeless or figure out how to try and make it work, maybe somedays your rent is a day late or just shy but the landlord can see that you are not going to quit even if it is shy of his expectation." Important note, that was on the spot, but for the third thing I told her is that "In life, you cannot take back your actions or words but can try to and in most cases that will make it worse, but you have only one chance. If I walked in here and disrespected you as I entered, it would be hard if not impossible to convince you that I am generally a good child even if we spoke on five other occasions afterwards. That would always be at the back of your mind no matter what." Or a better example which I gave after, "What if when I was young and stupid I commit a felony and ten or even twenty years later you look to hire me, the first thing you do is a background check and see that felony so just because of that, no matter how long ago it was it still negatively affects me. Because in a world of big data they need people to go through it or do they? In this big world, they use computers to turn you into a number to make a judgment but one thing they overlook is that unlike numbers people's "value" can change. I am not saying it always does but rather that it has the opportunity too." My final reason was if you looked at a perfect record, and all you saw was fours and fives on Yelp with nothing between one to three, would you still go there or how about if you saw a review changed because it was one star but the restaurant paid them to change it, would that still be a place you want to go, because I would not and whether you agree with me or not, the joys of this school is that it is an open enrollment school which means I have the final say on my choice, you can advise me but nothing more so no thank you, I will pass retaking this course at a lower level.

But back to the college part of this, she said that it would negatively affect me and also said that, "Much like a coin I come with two-sides and those that are there in times of weakness are the only ones that I can celebrate my strength with." I then stated, "So to those colleges that will say no, based on my one grade they will be missing out on an amazing student who will pay upfront and with no debt. Frankly, if the worst-case scenario happened I would go to a community college to get a special sheet of paper, it does not bother me if it is cheaper." Then I fully see the gears turning in her mind that this child is not normal and that he can express his points without being overwhelming or rude but rather vaguely intelligent and not as naive as I thought maybe I could try and speak to him rather than tell him something that he knows he has to listen to even though it would not matter because it is an open enrollment school. So I do not mind if schools say no based on my grades because I know I will work hard to be successful at whatever school I go to and, if nothing else, it can get some off my list, not like there is a shortage in trapping fresh adults in a lifetime of debt where interest is higher than what they are getting paid per year. But the point I am trying to share is that you are you with everything whether it is your temper or lack of historical knowledge it is you. There is no reason to butter yourself up to someone because even if you do not mention it they will most likely still see it no matter how hard you are trying to hide it anyway.

There are many beliefs about you whether you are your actions, thoughts, or words. But that is not something I am going to tackle, I believe "you" are your most actual self with no rules but the feeling in your heart. A world without a police force and justice would determine whether you are a good person or bad. In such a society, you would see your true colors. Because, sure you can steal something from someone but it is another to make your own; in one, nothing is created or destroyed from the world and in the other, the resources are transferred to make it but it is the same thing overall even though morality says otherwise. Though this mainly turns into ethical dilemmas based on our current society, one without societal influence, to begin with, is the true you, in my eyes. All ethical dilemmas answers will eventually all be right and wrong over time, it all just depends on how our society evolves and what problems arise and not to mention the solutions to them.

Perception

Wait...
Wait...
Fire!
Time the thing that keeps going,
No matter if you keep up with it,
Never stop or take a break.

Fire the ability to harm and to heal,
Use at your discretion,
What do,
What do,
But it isn't me nor you but id,
The inner you.

A battle between...

The devil on your back,
The angel on your shoulders,
Where choice is an illusion.

The battlefield so close,
So many,
All around,
Just open and look,
Don't be the blind man with perfect vision,
Be the man that does what he has to.

When you have a big task, the best thing is to break it down. For my task, that I want to complete with my friend is going to be long, complicated, and time-consuming and that is okay. The only way to complete large projects is to break it down into smaller bits until they are easily manageable, due to how the brain processes information and gives motivation. If you have a list of smaller tasks versus one big task, every little job that you complete gives you dopamine, which is your brain's happiness hormone. But this dopamine allows you to go further based on the fulfillment provided. For our project, money is not the reason but a product; we chose because we want to own more and because we can do more. Money is the wrong reason to start a project like this because, from my understanding, your bank account does not transfer after death, but at least the fulfillment will not go unappreciated rather than being left wanting more. But sometimes the solution to your project's struggles has already been accounted for by your subconscious, and you just need to wake up to reality. At least for the capital (money), there will always be more, but one's time can never be replaced or compensated. The legal system tries but you do now know what could have happened at that time, so I am going to spend mine the way I love and the lifestyle it provides. Innovation does not happen overnight or in one day; it is a process that takes hard work, a lot of time, and energy.

Yet if it is done in tiny phases it can make the whole project more manageable and more efficient that also includes a general increase in quality due to less "apparent pressure" causing you to be more alert. The modulation of items can allow for greater accuracy in general like release dates or durability because all you need to know is the weakest part to know one's strength. As technology improves we made things more modular because it comes out cheaper because in a perfect world we would not have manufacturing errors but we do here and with that would you rather throw away an entire laptop or just the battery and as people have more focused expectations and the desire to be different the market must adapt to make things more customizable, I believe it is a culture created by

Legos and I am not saying it is a bad thing but it is going to be different. Time and balance are critical things with life, but few have ever mastered it, and those proper priorities can change the outcome of an event that could increase infinitely better the chances of your project's success. The vision is the gate key of a project and not to be confused with a plan because there will always be more projects, but there will never be the same perception, those are known as competitors and what determines one from another.

At life's roots, perception is reality; in many cases, from vision to immediate wealth, it is all subjective and reality. For the most part, we all see colors, generally the full spectrum, but we never know if the color is truly the color it appears to be through our vision. Everyone sees color a little bit differently based on the qualities of one's eyes. As color only exists in your mind and not in the ordinary world without it. Our eyes see things typically upside down, but our brain flips the image before it is processed to get the world that we have today. Besides science, the only way to confirm a color was by using someone else yet we both do not see the same color and nor do we define it in the same way, an easy way to see this is when asking people the differences in the entire blue part of the spectrum or from red to orange to yellow. We know that things change over time so at what point we change what color we see?

There is a significant reason why you should never compare yourself to others, and that's because most things are relative or based on the person, a lot like color; the section above did have a purpose. Having transitional writing is a lot like a salesperson or some form of a manipulator because you are talking with yourself and dragging everyone with you, great speakers do this seamlessly and you begin to wonder how did we go from point A to point B, and the way to never run out of things to say is to create strong associations in your mind, let your mind be a slippery slope fallacy (The slippery slope is a logical fallacy where you challenge an opponent's argument and drag it through the worst-case scenario). The most relatable example is that Direct TV commercial if people even watch those these days, but it was something along the lines of, "Your bill goes up so you cannot feed your cat that month so your cat gets hungry and slashes your tires so you veer off the road into a ditch where you are now stuck in a wheelchair and cannot work, do not let your bill go up and get Direct TV." Even though it is almost impossible for this to happen it transitioned and flowed but to be able to do that seamlessly and with more reasonable ideas can allow you to go from talking able color to talking never being able to truly see something to talk about a logical fallacy and now on the verge of breaking with the fourth wall; like a rant that is not boring.

Due to pain and suffering also being relative, looking at someone else's life, and saying it is easy is most likely untrue with their life experience. Most people want to pick and choose what they would like from others and overlook the hard work it took to get there; after all, those who starve together thrive together. Life is not a stock you can buy and sell when it goes up or down. We all have peaks and troughs in our lives, and most do not pay attention to which stage they are relative to others when you are at rock bottom; that is the best time to shine the brightest. We share some similarities with sound waves here, when we are doing extremely well or terrible is when we cry the loudest yet when we are down we ask for more space although when we are doing the best we can be sure to share it with everyone to those of you that forgot that there are two types of sound waves, shame on you. What people do at the best of times often does not matter, but what they do at the worst is what differentiates you from everyone else.

Most people are judgers and critics, few are doers, but they are doing well later in life. Too many people try to find doers yet they search using "filetype: bored" and that is the thing to find those that are doing something. It has to be natural, networking, and not by putting out an ad because ads are looking for anyone but you are someone. When I can tell people are bouncing in between conversations with me and someone else I tell them to let me know when you want to talk with me and not with someone now because I have better things to do then talk to you when you are talking with someone. I am not the person that fills your loneliness when all else fails, but if you need help or want to trade ideas I'll be your guy. We are born in this amazing time where we can be what we want to yet we never learn what we want other than free time and money, many have begun to preach the turn your hobby into a job and that definitely works but certainly not for everyone especially when they hear what it costs to make that a reality. Doing the difficult sooner will make your life easier, but the opposite will make it harder, almost as if it is a savings account, and you just started at fifty compared to your brother that began at twenty. Sure at the time, he did not go out as much or did not have as fancy of a car, but now he owns and has paid off his house and can retire. But that's not you if you were average you would not be taking advice from a sixteen-year-old, right?

We all know or knew those people who were smart and I also know others who are jealous of that, specifically, those kids who took hard classes and never studied yet still managed to get a B with no effort. Sure there are a lot of factors that go into this but I tell my friends that are concerned about this that they should not worry about anyone else's marks. And that they should not care about them even though the competition is natural and always getting the lowest score can take a toll on you especially when it seems to come so easily to everyone else. I also give people an analogy, when a new rider gets on a motorcycle they want to keep pace with their friends but they do not have the experience to so when they try, they fall, compared to them just riding their own ride and being comfortable which is what riding is all about. Schools test knowledge based on position but learning is calculated by velocity and the quickness at which you learn something is based on acceleration; I guess that was two analogies

If they wanted to improve I told them to talk with those that got the highest score to learn about their secrets rather than going on their phone. I would say about ten percent of my free-time is spent on education all stuff, whether it be a youtube video or just reflecting on things, and even though I gave myself a very conservative number it can make a big difference, especially over summer, with the old saying, if you don't use it, you lose it. I am generally one of these people who can take really hard classes, get my B and move on, but what

I do ask them is if they are the type of person to click on a Youtube video about a subject they are taking or planning to take because it interests them. I do not study, I make my life my studying as I have interwoven it into my life. With me being one of these people it creates a problem for me. I will not know how to study when it comes to college if I never learn how and I also might not have a taste of the hard work needed to do certain tasks because I never needed to struggle that much.

So I give insight to hard-working students about the benefits of what they do compare to my current methods and others like us but the other thing that I failed to mention is that a key factor is a foundation. Learning especially in school is much like building skyscrapers, hopefully, and what I mean by that is you build one floor then you move up to the next but if you never learn key support for the next floor you will not be as secure and stable as those that have, thus equating to a lower grade. So to those that never learned Sin, Cos, and Tan they are bound to get a lower score in trigonometry and calculus because they do not know that fundamental skill. Another example could be not learning multiplication then having to square numbers it will be significantly less efficient. These people that put in the work and do not get the favored result I ask them are they mad at the fact they got a low score even when they put in the time?

I also tell them it does not matter, that score is in the past and there is nothing you can do about it except in rare situations wait, wait I meant common because when we get low scores, our parents see that and question us yet they see us studying so they then go to the teacher and because it is too much of a hassle to deal with parents, they gave and we get some form of a grade correction system; man sometimes I hate being born in this generation. Not to mention that it looks better on the teacher and school based on the average grades kids receive when in reality it does not mean much. So parents then do not yell at teachers but hey that is society a world where parents fight battles for their angelic children that are so perfect. The reason why it does not matter is the fact that if you tried for a good score you probably learned the content of which you studied and a test can try but ultimately falls short to accurately measuring true knowledge. So at least you absorbed the information to better yourself or to help later in life as those things you think may never come in handy just might since life is full of uncertainty, one day your economics major may suddenly shift to biomechanics and that information might be useful but because you were ignorant in high school will have to learn it once again. Though a lot like muscles it is infinitely easier to relearn something compared to the first time and many teachers call this review.

This is why I advise those that chase the grade to not study for the test but rather the test makers and the test itself, not the content. If you know the format at which questions are asked and how answers are so; you can make the test work for you and it can easily increase the accuracy of guessing from twenty-five percent to well over fifty with just learning the test. This is the major flaw with the College Board since they are producing so many questions for about thirty different subjects the format has to be consistent so they can make them easily so if you study the questions and ask what made the answer the right one, you might see a pattern. What signals did the creators' brains or programs use that made them similar. And that is how a test over the content of the entire year gets cheesed. You might consider the people that did this as smart but, really, they just took the box off their face and saw the true problem. Tunnel vision, a gift with such power but easily construed.

People see the end product and desire it but look at their hard work and to fill in your desires. Everyone says that they want to be that guy with all the cars and the big house but that is only because you have not experienced it. Think about it from a place of a rich child, he gets anything he wants, when he wants it and ends up starting trouble anyways. It is not because he is a troublemaker but rather it is the only way he can get that surge of chemicals; by doing things that are wrong since he never worked for his parents' money thus generating little satisfaction when spending it. That is also why it is so easy to waste other people's money and take more risks with it. Nothing separates it from your own except for the work but in to create it so it has less value in your mind. This is one of the reasons why when people open a business and start to pay for startup costs, they try to get as much as possible from the bank so it appears less likely to bite you since it is not your money and it is not the money you need to put the roof over your head causing less stress, even if Citibank might be mad at you if you lose it and you might not be able to travel for the rest of your life and even donate some of your debt to your kids as a nice passing away gift. The main thing is that you survive and that is what matters.

On the note of survival, I am going to talk about why kids truly and honestly decide to take themselves out and how they do it. We are going to talk about the difference between the parents' and child's perspectives to hopefully have someone do something about the real problem. This is not a one-day issue that will suddenly fix itself overnight, this a mindset one that we have neglected to stop.

So that one day you can trust that everyone will be there from the night before till the next day. So that one day it will not matter what you are feeling because you would then be able to say it out loud and not be told your response. But no matter if you had checked in on that person on that very day, it would not have made a difference, no matter how simple it seems to stop you would not have, no matter how impulsive it looked, it was not. I can say it was probably planned well in advance and with no one's knowledge. We look like antidepressant commercials, we live a lot like the ones where they have a stick with a smile over their face when they are with people but that mask is just that so when the party stops its back to business on the closing shop. That might have been the last straw but it was not the underlying problem and the problem may not be the parents but it might have something to do with their environment or any number of factors but all I can say is that I have never heard of someone fighting for their life just so they could end it (Maslow's Hierarchy of Needs).

At least eight hours a day is unaccounted for because of school and you do not know what goes on in there and you can only tell by word of mouth but there are always details left out. Parents that try to control their lives might as well be cigarettes and have their online grade book being the lighter.

I am going to put it this way, parents, when you are driving, are you always going at or below the speed limit, always? Sometimes you do not even know what it is and you guess and it turns out it is lower than what you thought so you slow down to meet it but anytime before that you could have been pulled over, you watch out grades books like hawks so that as soon as it falls below a certain mark you guys can give us crap even if it is not our fault, you do not believe us, you should know us and you should trust us but with technology trust seems to be a system that needs to be updated with cameras being in most people's houses and GPS' being in everyone's pockets location is seems to be a question of the past. Why trust when you can find out right here, right now; some say that the point in a relationship when you have to go through a girl's phone is the day it is over. I have to agree when a company is more discreet about your privacy than your SO (significant other) there is a problem, the same thing can be said about your child especially the good ones, you need to let us fail on our own and experience it on our own. Sometimes we may fail a test or two, or maybe not do an assignment here or there but we do not deserve to be pestered about it as soon as we walk in the door because you already got a notification and your life is so sad that you have to stalk your child to know they are doing the right thing. We just want you to understand and give us some space and trust us, note this does not apply to those that have proven that they cannot be trusted but to those that never did anything wrong, give them the space that they deserve. Cops are not always watching you so why are you doing it to your kids, you want to prepare them for life yet ultimately make it unrealistic. Unless you have done some sketchy things, and in that case, you know what's best and how to prepare your child for those special circumstances but the "normal" people of this world act like insurance. By that I mean they check their record quarterly unless they want to talk about it on their own accord, which leads down two paths and both serve a purpose. If it is good then they know that it will most likely be just to get you off their back and it will most likely drop. But if it is bad they need help, to admit that they are doing poorly and will take the associated consequences because there is no possible way to "survive" that and they have to do it on their terms.

Kinda like the ultimate choice they make: they want to go out on their terms. Since life is meaningless overall and the only reason you do not feel that way is because of our need to survive and those big businesses creating jobs and competition, other than that there is no reason other than what one feels but there is no end goal of life. We live, we die, we get lost in history, and we become something new bound to repeat. Businesses are never expected to live forever so why do think we will. But with life being meaningless so is death if you think about it and from our current knowledge, it is just like before we were born.

But back to the problem that solves itself, you as a parent have to let your child live a little so. Whatever classes they get make them stick with it, teach them to work with what they have rather than working with what they want, as long as nothing illegal happens. And that, "Mom science is too hard I want to drop it." Your answer is no, the class is not what you wanted; so what? What are you going to do about it, learn to like it, or; choose to suffer? You will not be able to take things as easily as and change them unless there is an actual reason. Especially since no one cares about you unless you give them a reason to like you. Teaching that rising to the occasion is a way to grow is important, in life you need those on the fly moments to improve; the truest innovation is not planned for. Where comfort is obtained is when growth stops and if they cannot rise let it show on their report card or their record as a reminder of their limits.

Some say shaming is wrong but it works only for fixable things, like shaming someone based on something race or gender is a no-no but I believe shaming based on muscle/weight or skill in something is fair game because those things are not set in stone and you can improve upon them once you decide to work at it. All the time in life I get people saying I am short, thank you I never noticed I'll make sure to look up to the mirror to see how tall I am but overall I am okay with it because being short is great. I can disappear into crowds, movie-style and I also have way more movement options available if I ever need to use them for if I need to fit into a tight space. Although it is not fair to denounce me based on something set in stone like height.

Something that I do despise is when people give you advice on the easy way out, now this did not happen, I repeat, this is one hundred percent made up and no word in this is true. But I was in line at Staples talking with my mom about something less than important and the cashier says that his son was small like me but they decided to put him on growth hormones and now he is over six feet tall and to not worry about it as I will grow like him. Now my mom did not catch this at first till once we were in the car I had her repeat his words out loud and then she realized how contradictory his words are with his previous actions. Like I see his point and I agree but you do not say something along the lines of my son was fat and now after surgery he is skinny, I know you will slim down one day. That is just not how that works, even though he was trying to be nice, I have to give him that but make sure your thoughts and actions align for it to be believable or even make sense. But to those that have said that I am weak repeatedly throughout my life, I have started lifting and I look like I have the pretty good definition to my physique compared to just being skinny and based on the body type I had to work harder to put on that muscle than most but I do not care I wanted to get stronger for them to stop saying it. It was not bullying even though some may see it that way it was just the motivation and the truth. Those people that said it, decided to because it would make them feel better about themselves until they saw a difference and then they said nothing as I passed them in halls to talk with them. Knowing that I get the last laugh every time I see them.

You can judge me here but I believe suicidal thoughts are normal, within reason. Let's say you are cleaning the house and do not feel like doing it then, it is okay if the thought comes in saying what if I put this butter knife into the outlet. Like the thought can happen but it is not like you are serious or going to it is just like a way to pass time. I also think mental depressions are a part of life and are not a problem as long as they do not last and linger for let's say a month but my rule is three days. I will fall into these phases that I call cosmic depression which is extreme existential nihilism where everything is meaningless and I wonder why I am here and if I was better off dead because of the butterfly effect and just a bunch of thoughts on a massive scale about existing where I feel nothing emotionally. Or how no matter how great I am, I will eventually be lost to never be spoken or thought of again and even the thought that if everything is life is a walking contradiction. Like in English, where we are to read complex texts where we need to infer the answer yet we are told to write with direct connections to make it easier on the graders because they are short on manpower and do not care and this can be felt when it feels like a random number generator determines your score. Why care about your work or if we are told to infer all we would need to show logical reasoning in every situation is due to survival because that is why we do anything no matter how deep the rabbit hole of fallacious reasoning it eventually leads there, no matter the fallacies used to get there.

From the outside world, I have a problem because I can think of and see the possibilities and as society tries to make people appear like clones, they all say that I need to fix my life like a broken tool. We enter schools as question marks yet come out as periods, seems like school takes the opposite day as lifetimes. Because society covers reality with expectations they are all over the place from

Disney movies to social media. No one ever mentions those hard conversations with parents. No one mentions that the simple things are made to be a hassle to achieve certain goals psychologically. There is always an easier way but that is not how the world works. It is based on money from the difficulty of the task.

Getting back on track, we kill ourselves because we feel like we will be killed so we might as well do it on our terms. We believe that surviving is now impossible either due to a mistake or otherwise, we cannot handle the reality because we were never exposed to a tough reality, that is not our life. So when it comes we drop life like a class, maybe next life I will complete it. The American dream is lost within us, the passion is there kinda but not really and the "hard work" is there but only within those quotes. Outside of those it does not exist, we do not understand the grind, the strain, we can truly take. We stop at fifty percent because that is what we are comfortable with and used to. Those that say they are busting their butt in most cases do not have anything to show for it or it was not worth it and so we do not allow ourselves to get hurt like that.

Those that play sports only with the time on the field are players, the legends are the ones that do it in every waking moment and those are truly few and far between; the hustlers. When you need them you think they are normal because they try to appear that way but when they break their walls down you see the work they put in every day and you think about me complain about this cramp but they are swimming for well over eight hours a day on two different teams and taking an English class for the smartest Juniors but they are doing it as a Sophomore. You see that they are so busy they cannot even stop to think about overworking or depression. They simply do not have time for it, they just see it and see the goal and fire. Nothing more, nothing less; no one can stop them unless they choose to. I believe Darwin was a pretty smart guy with the survival of the fittest, those who wack themselves are not the people we need to improve the world we live in.

We see something on the surface but is that enough for you, it is not for me. I have my own five senses so I am not going to take someone's word on what is best for me without trying it my way because ultimately I know me the best. Everyone has an opinion but who -actually- acts on it, as they say, you can never just find do' ers on accident. They either come to you or you find them, not like others where they just wait for something to happen and react to it. Will you be the person that learns something because they want to or because the market for it is booming? People are no the system of law they can be proactive but that is so much harder because when something happens someone creates an opinion which ultimately causes others to form the same belief as that is how news shows work they look at something that happened and give their two cents for you to take and spread to others that you know. You take others' thoughts and use them as your own. Social conditioning is a perception in itself, a business suit is just fancy clothing to make others think that you are important but other than that and an inside pocket provides no actual value.

People think that me writing a book is a good thing, at least for the people that know me but from what I have noticed it is the hardest thing I have had to do. Life makes annoyances happen at really convenient times so much so that I believe I can turn my life into a sitcom and rewrite the entire first book which was based on a true story and just turn into a comedic masterpiece. My first attempt at writing a book got laughed off in the literary stage and cringed so no, other than my close friends my first attempt did not make it because they even shut it down. I got through ten pages of it and it was shut down. I thought it was the greatest thing and they humbled me and made me realize that it was not a product I could be proud of but with more laughs, kinda like that kid in the gym for the soccer ball even though it was stationary. Although they did not tell me how I could improve, they told me it was not good which could have been nicer; but, it worked, it made me refine my craft even though till writing this I never thought I would have written a book. Now I watch as they call and message in group chats and I need to say I'm writing or editing because I need to be even though I want to be hanging out with them and in the same breath I had maybe an hour or two before which I could have worked on it but I used it as my time. I did have to give up on something and right now as I wait for my book trailer to render in 4k and with sixty frames per second I cannot join them but now I physically cannot so this is a time where I can do essentially nothing on my laptop except browser the internet. For thoughts not aware of what rendering is, it is where you take the edited video and process it to make a seamless new video. You can never win but you can also never lose the game where every step lands you in the same footprint of the last yet it looks like you are going somewhere.

Potential

Tick-Tock,
Time moves whether you do or not,
It's always used but never saved,
With never being seen but felt,
Silent   alone   but   supportive   together,
providing context with each scene.

Never knew when it started,
But will never end,
No specific day,
But give it a month,
It will change,
They always do,
It once stayed longer,
But only once.

But it takes two to tango,
And I am only one,
I want my imagination to be my reality,
Seems to be so far but others can only see it
getting closer,
As if its a goal that I keep bumping further,
Just out of reach from me,
Now it is not squandered but is delayed.

Others look in and see the best and hope for
it,
It's not like their wrong, but there is so much
more,
As it takes two to tango and I am only one,
With every bump making it slip further into
oblivion.

Everyone thinks intelligence is one of the highest standards to hold and judge someone by, but some fantastic qualities are currently undervalued, the main one is work ethic. I like to say I am a pretty intelligent guy but not over the top to a genius level, but in most cases, hard work is a vessel from A to B, but intelligence is just the speed limit. Luckily I learned this early in my life, but some of you might not have had that epiphany yet. It does not matter how smart you are, compared to doing it day in and day out; hard work prevails over talent. Sure, it can be frustrating at times when someone looks at it, and it clicks with them, but they do not receive any fulfillment for that since they did not undergo any struggle. Because of the lack of apparent effort, their brain valued it as nothing special, but that in a closed environment when competition or others are introduced, it can change the apparent value of the struggle based on the people that they are around. I am only going to give two examples of this, so take notes and re-read. I was in AP physics one, (yes there are more), and I finally figured out how to use one of the forms to solve a couple of problems, so that flood of dopamine came in. Then my neighbor (from the perspective of the classroom still) had already finished it, and what I mean by that was the entire twenty-nine-page packet was finished causing my stream or neurochemicals to slow because it made the accomplishment appear less then it is. All and all, my brain now labeled it as not so important based on my surrounding environment, but without it, it would be considered a feat. Well, I guess it was one example with just a change in circumstance rather than separate ones.

I am a kid that does not study for school, I get "good" grades, but nothing near perfect, and I know that I could be close, but I have no reason to. Some say, "what about college" and my response is,

"There are people worse than me that get accepted, and now there is a community college, I get the same slip of paper no matter what, I might as well use my time in something I deem wise." So I do not work hard when it comes to school, and while some of my friends do the opposite, spending their time studying and can sometimes get better marks than me, but they see it as a priority. But I believe it is short-sighted so you will only see me around them on test day or to compare scores, but I would not waste my time throwing wilding crazy business ideas as they are not concerned with that at the moment. I believe that studying is for people that are concerned with the present even though they are preparing for the future but it is normally so close that by the time they take their head out of that textbook it is time to take the test rather than devoting that time to something that lasts beyond school or past the next ten to twenty years of their lives. They are like the day traders of stock market investors. Comparison of two or more unlike objects leads to a bias of either an attack on one or an overt defense of another without taking it all into account and not even taking into account Einstein's theory of Relativity. Which states everything in the universe is relative; in layman's terms, no two people feel the same pain. In English that would be like trying to convince a die-hard person of any scale of the political scale to change their viewpoints, most times they will not even process the opposition's perspectives. It will be like men's hearing, even though, no matter the outcome it will still be the same. Politics is all about being opposites on insignificant problems to make regular people feel like they change the course of the country in reality what was will be. But back to those friends, they are not smarter than me; they worked harder and put in the effort, and so we both have mutual respect for one another, both wanting what we can't have with our values. That sounds a lot like our society, where the rich are missing a human part of their lives called happiness, and the poor are losing money. Everyone wants a better position, but what do you give up for the improvement, most times you do not know or get to choose.

Now people hate crime but only if it happens to them, a "victimless crime" is one where everyone wins but then why would there be a law against it? People think that stealing from "the man" only has winners until they realize that they are only raising the price of insurance and taxes but no one ever follows the paper trail to notice that. But most people are paid for about forty hours a week and yet only work for three hours a day which equates to fifteen hours a week because most people do not work all seven days of the week. But with that, those that are paid by the hour are stealing from the company for every hour that is used walking up and down the sales floor while there are no customers or when there is no shipment to be moved into the back room. But people make sure they are clocked in for that time even though they are not working for it and all it does is hurt those that do not do that.

Take a step back in time, to the Mayans and the sacrificing of goods to appease the gods; they sacrificed the food that they good enjoy for the protection that they offered (From their perspective). They did not give up their scrapes or toxic foods; they got first to pick at what they wanted, leaving the village with what was leftover. That is how sacrifice works, you choose what you want, and you give up some of the most important things at the moment to get what you chose. You cannot double-dip; you cannot pick both the sacrifice and the goal, that is not how it works, and that is not how a compromise works. So if you are willing to make sacrifices every day to get what you want a day in and day out, that is irreplaceable and invaluable for life. Then there those people who like to complain bring everyone around then down. Do not let others affect you; it is hard. When friends, family, or even strangers that only see your posts turn their back on you because they do not believe, you know you down to your core if you genuinely believe in yourself and pour your heart and soul into it, everyone will see it after they made a mistake giving up truly before it has started. Just like me right now writing this book, "your sixteen what could you know the world" or "you cannot write a book on that" and my favorite, "really, do you think it will sell, no one even knows you." To that, I give them my final product, and I let it stand on its own two feet, I believe that I did everything I could to make this the best possible product, and whether or not it is bought does not concern me, after all, I did not write this profit or fame but for thoughts that do read it treats it as a bible or the problematic situations with the direct stress. This book is the standard I am going to hold myself to going forward till I go six feet under.

The art of taking risks is just like any other skill is probably the most undervalued in society, even with its potentially infinite benefits. Everything we know can come from a chance, generally jumping into the unknown to see where it leads. Every single choice that we do not one-hundred percent knows the outcome is one that involves risk no matter how small. Risk itself is not inherently good nor bad but based on perspective like many things. What is worse, ignoring the potential of exploring something based on the associated risk or taking it and failing? When someone mentions risk, and the chances are that you think of it as a gamble and with an external locus of control, not realizing that it can be altered if you alter your mindset. When you change your mindset, you change your result, and that can either be positive or negative, depending on the said change. As someone distinguished/famous once said, "The greatest power you give up is by not believing you have any." In many cases, perception is the reality it could be directly or indirectly, such as I believe I am confident, so I appear to be, no matter my body or other belief, I am optimistic, so I am.

We have all been told to fake it till you make it, but that is because most just straight cannot when you have a typical problem, but you aren't an average person, the solution provided suddenly does not work as effectively for you. Sometimes you already have everyone fooled, but that does not make it your reality. Schools are built not to value the skills needed for life or real-world success, no matter how much they say otherwise. People say lying is wrong, but it is how it is used in one's definition of the word "bad." But society has labeled it as something terrible yet bluffing or concealing if different as if the use of a different name changed people's feelings about it. The need to look sleek and still fit is a growing struggle generally not limited by time but rather the money to do so. It is an endless cycle of the mass following few, similar to how people chase money but thought people that change fashion trends take the risk of being alienated, for the reward of changing society even though it is generally for money. The only reason this concept works is because of social peer pressure and the need for people to be accepted even with everyone who has different tastes in style and goals. Some people like to be the center of attention, so they choose and like to wear flashier outfits compared to thoughts who want to blend and be silent.

My taste personally falls within one of these four colors: black, grey, white, and navy. That is my ideal choice unless I am feeling primarily extraverted then I will go for a maroon red. Even though it might be annoying, it -definitely- takes way too much effort to color coordinate outfits every single day, not to mention making the entire laundry process more complicated than it has to be; I enjoy a simple life. Without colors, you most likely would not even have to iron assuming you hang/fold them immediately and forget doing multiple loads or giving certain clothes special treatment i.e. steaming.

Before relatively recent years, fashion trends were the make or break of your status in high school, with people being judged, but now most of that open prejudice is still there but rather locked into our internal monologue. The difference in how we treat people based on the "uniform" is immense. It can justify people stealing television since people thought that the thieves were a part of a maintenance team and in most cases, you do not even need to show any form of identification because no one thinks about it in that complex of a light. Till it is your money that is being wasted, that is when everyone cares, only when it happens to them, but that's too late. Whether it is statistics or engineering, any field that you have not been in has different protocols that you might not even know about because you do not think of it such as that example of theft. The art of stealing is so complex that there is a giant gap between those that are petty thieves that need a little extra cash to get buy compared to those that do it as a day job. And I recommend you listen and watch videos of already caught criminals and notice common takeaways or behaviors because patterns or lack of can save a life.

Keep in mind that eyes are the windows to the soul and hands are the voices of intent. Criminals are still people with a variety of skill sets so learn from them the best way to not lose something is to talk with those that take it. Most are likely to treat people with baggy and ripped clothing with less respect and authority then other people and that is based on observation but even though they might look like that it might be wise to ask just in case because if someone can lose money they will often be able to show you the opposite and knowing those people, they have probably been through so much that you might change your priorities to something that matters.

A mini social experiment was run where a homeless man was begging for money and a man in a suit begging for money because the homeless man looked the part he acquired significantly more handouts and even a couple of meals some people have been able to abuse this have a corner where beg even though they are not homeless and some can make up to and over one hundred thousand dollars a year. But even though that sounds good it still has its equal cost and that is the toll it takes on your morals, because they know it is wrong yet does it anyway. The same thing for the guy in the suit: he had more authority with his clothing causing fewer people to give time handouts, especially when it looks like your employees are giving you money. But in reality, a boss would not be a boss without people under him to manage so they are feeding his paycheck. Another deterrent to add to the other details was the fact that for an action to go through swiftly and accurately in the brain your thoughts and actions need to align but they were not in this case. As someone was begging in something that looked like money which created cognitive dissonance within the participants and in such a fast-paced world like this one they did not even react to it because they simply could not decide on an action.

We all have heard the saying, "give a man a fish he will be fed for a day, teach a man to fish he will be fed for a lifetime." There is some level of truth to that in the world of yourself and business. What I mean by this is that it is one thing to do something and just replicate the motions and an entirely different thing to learn it. Almost like the debate between memorization and learning; one can memorize something but be limited and confined to that one specific thing. But if you learn it, you can build it, and teach it; this can easily be explained with an example with cooking if you choose to memorize you have to look at the recipe every single time or make it but not be able to accommodate for different sizes or changes in individuals personal taste in flavors. For those that learn it, they can adapt their recipe on the fly for the audience that one is cooking for, whether for kids that want a less spice based taste or for an adult who seeks that more mature/in-depth taste, almost to self validate that they are an adult.

Portraying it from a business perspective, if you choose to teach people in the business world you will find that you will do the jobs of thoughts lower than you less often if you end up teaching them how to do it themselves. You cannot expect someone to do something that they never learned and there is no reason to assume that they learn it, you do not know their life gives them that benefit. The next issue that arises is, what about that person that you keep trying to teach but never learns because they never truly have to; and to that, I say that you need to find a better student. But if this instance repeats -time and time again- it seems as if it is about time that you look back and do an introspective vision of your recent past and think to see how you could do better. The true masters of anything never truly stop learning; after all, they are the masters and the students in their minds.

Learning never stops no matter your age or skill because the true best will never stop growing, they have gone through too much to stop now. You know you are at the top of anything when you can find and solve one of the problems that are holding you back by yourself. True mastery is the dedication of never stopping the process of growth and learning. It generally goes with; recognizing, advancing, solving, and teaching; this is a very broad brush and this process can take anywhere between a week to even up to a year depending on the skill. But every step is important for different reasons with, yet again, various levels of significance. We will remember this acronym as R.A.S.T.; if you do not see how I got those letters to look back up to the four words list. For the intelligent people of society, RAST is a radioallergosorbent test that is a blood test using a radioimmunoassay test to detect specific IgE antibodies, to determine the substances a subject is allergic to. Properly using and applying these principles will make you allergic to being inefficient.

You need to be able to recognize your problem to improve, thoughts who think they are too perfect to have had a problem either are the problem or are the ones with less actual intellect then the amount perceived. This leads back to the Dunning Kruger effect that states in laments term the dumber you are the less likely to realize you are dumb. But there is an exponential curve on this meaning true idiots will know that they are lacking in the knowledge department and the same can be said for the upper echelon of society. They will know their lack of knowledge and not pretend as they do, due to our world's mysterious nature and general lack of understanding even though we know so much already. Intelligent individuals on a topic do not pretend to also not waste others' time as again it is the one thing in life that we cannot get more off. Time is the world's premium currency yet can't find a credit card to purchase more than they, yet keep spending it on items on things that do not have value outside of oneself.

The second stage in a cycle of mastery is advancing, when solving a problem you need to grow in more ways than one to solve it. Since your brain is a muscle it would be wise to treat and train it that way. Most people head to the gym to either get into better shape or lie to themselves to believe that they are doing something from just being there. Let me explain that with a more personal analogy when I wanted to find something to occupy my time with over the summer, I found myself looking at motivational videos and such to get the mentality and mindset for when I find my spark. The video told me that there is a difference between being busy and being productive and that lit a flame in my mind as if I finally found the secret to life. So when I would have the same classes with friends yet some if not most would have homework yet I would not. I wondered why and this made so much sense when they had time they worked on it with distractions and very inefficiently. It is not like I am a genius but fairly efficient because I do not want to spend my time doing homework all-day. It's a choice, yet most do not see it that way, who would want to spend time doing redundant work? So they try to get out of it like; let me grab a snack, some water; Instagram break; all these excuses. I, personally, had homework sixteen days during my freshman year, twelve days during my sophomore, and I am at three days for my junior year. Most of my friends have homework every day, without fail. Before you jump to the conclusion no I am not taking easy classes, all honors and four AP's (advanced placement) adding to a total of seven classes. Nor am I socially awkward at least not more than any other guy. It is that I see it that we have eight hours in school and that is About four-hundred and eighty minutes of learning and work time. That is what it is there for, so when I wake up I have planned out my workload for the day in my head about how much goofing off time I have during the day. RAST will again make you allergic to being unproductive.

The third stage -and by far the most valued stage according to society- is solving the problem, this is where the results happen. Notice how this is not the last stage much like newer business models this includes sustainability rather than getting results and starting back at square one because what will happen is that solving the problem will take a lot longer than necessary with the final step but I am getting ahead of myself, can you tell I do that a lot? But here you take all of your observations and tests and apply them to generate the result that you want. Remember that your actions directly generate your result like an X, Y chart from Algebra when you want a different result you cannot just expect it to happen out of thin air but you. As you should remember the definition of insanity is doing the same thing over and over again and expecting a different outcome. In most cases implementing and activating the solution is going to be the hardest part, so if you think step one or two is difficult, it doesn't get easier it gets harder, kinda reminds me of life. You did not grow just to make the weight lighter if you would not do it at the gym there is no reason to do it with your life. We all want it easier. This is the easiest if you look at it long term, as long and short term is generally an endless battle, but if it takes so long would you not like the long-term solution. See it is easier to say that than to actually do it because the short-term rewards feel good at the moment but a long-term decision keeps giving until you no longer need it to. I think you can come up with examples on your own for this one.

There is no point in learning something if you are not going to share it since human beings are social animals. We have a fundamental need to talk and what better than something you just learned as you can be boosting others' knowledge and at the same time collect happiness from your accomplishment. Also when you share an idea you can have others build off of it to either make it their own or make it better than you could even imagine but good ideas spread a lot like good actions, start with a drop and create a ripple that becomes a tsunami and that is how technology startups like Rivian started. With an idea and then as he mentioned it others believed till they got the money to make it a reality because people believed and heard about his idea. The best idea is one worth sharing, which is why the TED (Technology, Entertainment, Design) organization was founded, to promote ideas to others in a non-commercial way in a capitalist society. When you know something that someone has not realized it is your job to educate them to improve society. Though you should only teach those that have an affinity for the said thing because you will just waste your time educating your family that does not care but states that they will support you because let us be honest for a minute not many people care for your craft as much as you do and many of those that think they support you it will most likely be in spirit. But if a random guy on the street loves the idea and starts to help no matter how inefficient or mentally incapable, tell them because maybe just maybe they will help improve it to new heights previously foreign to your view. You never know someone's thoughts or thought processes unless you give them a scenario.

Just remember RAST to keep moving forward and solving problems. In the gaming world, RTS (real-time strategy) players already have a term for this and that is min-maxing where they find something like a skill and dedicate themselves to it and make everything revolve around it. In this case, your craft is in the top five priorities always, it stays in your mind as you sleep, you mention it to others and you constantly try to learn more. It is the type of thing that you will work more than required and do the optional work as required to further better yourself or the thing itself. These people that fail and may fail often know that if they keep trying statistically it is a higher chance then doing nothing. Since it is based on the biggest limiting factor in humanity, time, they are statically more likely to complete it if they choose to then if it were forced upon them. Not to mention the fact that it takes the same amount of work to get something done but if you work ahead you get to choose when and how much work to do within the constraints set for oneself.

Personal story here, where I can guarantee you will judge me but let me get into it. So I want a motorcycle and that's great and all -even my parents are willing to buy the equipment and bike- but then all I need to do is pass the MSF (Motorcycle Safety Foundation) course which is where they teach you how to ride. In the end, if you pass they give you your endorsement which is a thing on your license that states you legally cannot kill yourself or someone else while operating a motorcycle, a lot like a driver's license. But all of that is not too relevant, here is where it gets interesting and yes it does. I never actually learned how to ride a bicycle, that was an issue that my parents said I would need to do to get one. I am not the child of rich parents even though I may be spoiled. I do kind of have a reason for not learning to ride till sixteen but the majority do say I am not spoiled no matter what you think. My excuse for not learning to ride was that when my parents got divorced the parent that I learned with no longer had a bike and I never thought to do it with the other; so it just sat there collecting dust. That sounds like a terrible excuse but whatever, so after they told me this I looked around my neighborhood for a bike that worked and luckily found one. It was a rusted cherry-red bike with tires flatter than a crushed soda can. But on day one we got it ready to ride, with it oiled and tires inflated then I started just by pushing myself and asking my dad when we would be done then he said at least an hour. So I decided to not ask and focus with just trying and with a lot of sweat and fails I got to two revolutions and no balance and two hours later I fall hard on my thumb filled/pushed it not allowing me to put pressure on it so I stopped for the day over an hour past the time if I kept asking. Then the next day I got to ride in a straight line and never bothered about asking how long because I wanted this motorcycle and they said I needed to learn so I do not know how long, how many falls, or how much sweat I kept going I never saw me riding a bike but I saw that motorcycle and if this was the work I needed to do I had to do it no matter the pain I was still in because of thumb. Then day three came and I could basically ride with the occasional fall of miss judgment but I could ride just fine and my dad saw this and said, "Look you did it and you did not paint my car red." I would never have learned to ride if it was not a requirement and every day I made progress and I tried forgetting the potential judgments from pasting neighbors as would occasionally see me fall.

You know those people that you believe can do anything they set their minds to. NO, Karen not your kids; I mean actual people. But you try to help these people, you give them resources, your thoughts, and even some advice yet they do not help themselves. Like they are constantly in the process of saying things but never actually doing anything. It is like they are in a permanent state of cognitive dissonance constantly saying they want to do this and that but their actions mean nothing. Like the sheer words they utter give authority, maybe that works for everyone else but true authority is given to you not seized like weed at an airport. That is the same person that will tell people to be quiet so they can speak compared to listening and helping them and their ideas. There are two types of leadership, the one who forces it and it is just the most aggressive or the one where everyone knows who the leader is but at the same time he relies on trust to get things done. People who have power should not always use it to get things done, because that is not a leader but a dictator.

Do you want to be known for your position or for what you actually did? Because if you become a teacher, that desk is not yours but rather it is for whoever is in that position yet many think it is there for them when it is there for those who hold their title. Normally with being a teacher you get respect. It is expected of the students to give respect unconditionally, and teachers are supposed to do the same thing back yet some do and others do not. I am a fan of judging people based on their actions and I am also a person that believes that you make your bed. Other than a government official, no one gets my respect just for being there. If their actions deserve respect they will get it but if they do not then they do not get it. I have done this to teachers and assistant principals but the reason I exclude military officials is because if they do not like you they can choose to never let you see the light of day again and even though I am a night person I would like the option to see the stars or to see the sunrise now and then.

One day my dad asked me why I never waved at the assistant principal in the morning, and I said it is because her actions already said something so I choose to give her the same respect she gave me. I do not see why I should give her special treatment. The school would be just fine without her and it would be one less person to shake hands with at our graduation. Note that she started doing this as soon as the principal said that this was his final year. Now even though I paint her like a bad person, she is alright but compared to the notions of her position her actions are dubious at best. Now the different form of this happened with my mom where my mom wanted to know who I saw standing in line ahead of us and it was my guidance counselor and sure enough, I let her know but she questions my apparent disrespect to her (guidance counselor) and says that it is unacceptable so I say imagine if all debates were like this, being lectured about a side you do not even know, you may think you know but you do not. Imagine if one person disagreed with you, you just got shut down. Just because you need to tell people all day what to do, because some of them seem to mess up the simplest of tasks, does not mean that you have the right to yell at me. You cannot think of a valid point to overturn my ideas. Now a key point of why I am not fond of my guidance counselor is that every year we get a new one. It is like hi, how are you and what is something interesting about you, oh wait I am leaving without notice, bye. Oh why hello, let me know if you have any concerns *leaves.* But this one, in particular, was acting like a used car salesman just trying to get me into something I did not want to be bothered in and because I already know who to use that approach in swaying people I was able to not fall into that pitfall which seems to work very often for young kids. I give my respect to those that deserve it but to cut that story short I just got even more stonewalled by my mom and that was that. There is something about aging that makes one more set in their ways and unable to change.

Solution

We all try,
We all have a place to go and people to see,
We all want to come home,
Ask yourself,
Is my want more than yours.

I want to come home,
I will come home,
I fight for a home to come back to,
It is not given but earned,
I work for tomorrow,
As it will be harder tomorrow than today,
That every day I will be losing,
Losing the war of attrition.

There are those waiting,
The ones I have met those I will meet,
I made a promise,
Not today,
Not today,
I will not break it,
Today is not an option,
There are many days but not the same as today,
Whether it be good or bad,
It is mine,
I have,
I am more than today,
Yesterday,
And tomorrow,
What sets must rise,
It may not be the same but it still rose,
It is still here,
The simple leaves the biggest footprint.

The world in which we live is backward, and it is in the best interest of everyone to fix it before it gets worse. I do hope everyone remembers basic human history, with men being the primary hunters and the rest being gathered. These civilizations were mainly known as hunter-gatherer civilizations, but what most people do not know is that the meal was dominated by what the gathers collected rather than the meat that was pulled in. After all the closer to the source you get, the more authentic it is.

A simple example could be the game of telephone, where one person says something to the next and so on until the end and checks to see if it is the same. This is also accurate with nutrients since the middle man or animal does not have the chance to absorb any of the resources of the plants. It is estimated that about ninety percent of our diet in that period was made of plants, and there is no arguing that it was a time when humans were at their peak physique.

Though this is not the only thing that we have backward, but rather the entire business world. In our society, putting ourselves above others makes us gain, but isn't that the definition of power-hungry or tranny. It seems best done in the military because risking yourself for the betterment of others earns you medals and not the other way around. But the thing is in life that there are so many people that want to help, but it requires one to help someone else beforehand and suck up your pride and help. It takes a lot to ask, why do you think men never ask for help at the store because it is not easy and problems aren't simple; they are what came from the simple.

Future-proofing is solving problems that haven't happened yet, and odds are it is harder because if it were easy, it really would not be much of a problem. But when a problem does arise with gossip or any conflict, make sure you go to the source and not the messenger because the source can influence and make. Even when you think no one is listening, everyone has a subconscious, whether it is the devil on their shoulders or the angel on their back, but their listening; always. The most substantial strikes happen internally. In this next section note that I am not defending or approving of anything I just formulated an argument to what seemed like the underdog side.

Beef should remain in burgers since the potential long term health effects are still unknown. It is believed that meat causes chronic adverse health effects, but there is no research on the plant-based alternative, which could be just as bad if not worse than meat products. Sometimes it is better to deal with the devil we know than the enemy of the unknown.

Mainly based on the number of sales it has gotten recently in restaurants since it is believed to be healthier, but truth be told, we have no idea whether that is reality or not. For the most part, money strains a company's eyes and blurs them, leaving money as the only thing in their vision, and then things get corrupted. The integrity companies have for their food products will most likely take a backseat when some are making upward of four-hundred percent more in revenue. However, that does not mean profit, in this case, seems to, at the very least, have a strong association.

The ingredients of a burger are not the problem but rather a way to place blame. Eating anything in the human body without proper moderation is going to have health effects. Generally, the people that do eat fast food a lot eat it way more than their bodies could handle, and that is not going to change by renaming it and making it with different ingredients. Pigs are going to be and stay that way, but they need a reason to justify it to themselves and others rather than looking at the actual source. Granted, it is human nature to take responsibility for the good and leave the bad ostracized. There is no reason to change the materials within a burger if it is just going to create the same problems due to people's inability to take care of themselves. Maybe soon the blind will be able to see; if only ignorance was a crime. With a plant-based alternative, there are more things people could be allergic to based on the various amounts of plants they need to splice to make this thing.

In life, there are the rare exceptions to rules, and in the science world, we call them theories, work as a good rule of thumb but might not be able to work in every situation you can throw at it and in more times than not in life there are fewer laws to situations. Most times when people fund a company it is because they want to make money but that should never be the end-all especially when in a leadership position. One should always try to make themselves a part of something bigger than themselves because then money will follow in most cases and you gain self-sustainability in your happiness. When the vision is the priority certain things matter less and less and others get stronger in order to build a community. A community is any group of people that have something in common, not just in the housing context even though that is where it comes from.

Chasing profit has unintended consequences in most cases that people do not see until it is too late but could have been avoided if they sacrificed their greed. The Thing that puts this into perspective is thinking about what you can take to the grave and what I mean by that is what you can take with you after death. In many cases you cannot take money, so why keep chasing it just to die with it unspent. Having a project that matters not only to you but to others will create innovations the likes of which most have never experienced. Prime example Tesla was not founded by Elon Musk on the sole premise of making money; it wanted to shake up and innovate the car industry with affordable luxury electric cars. For that matter all of Elon's companies we found with a vision or goal in mind and not for the idea of making money. The manual evolution of human beings is the single most rewarding thing because you know for a fact that it is helping people and some may rely on it and that would not have happened if it was not for the creator.

Technology will constantly be improving no matter what any individual chooses and it is our choice to adapt to it. But as we learn our optimism gets proved wrong time and time again as if the best-case scenario is now labeled impossible reality. The statement provided appears to be very true and accurate, that knowledge is pain due to imaginations, the complexity of life, and simplicity of none.

Imaginations can change this and manipulate them in such ways that in most cases reality cannot replicate. The happiness of people gets channeled into their subconscious whether they like it or not, people's best intentions are for good and not harm. So it would reasonably be assumed that the best outcome would be formed in the clouds of your head only to be transpired in a less sunny way in actuality but that gave the motivation. Another example of this is, for most of us when we were kids we did not think of it as sad or difficult but rather this amazing thing and we wanted to grow up so fast and as we got older like into our teenage years we learned more about the truth and challenges that came with it. Someone put it best, "the dream is free but the hustle is sold separately." This quote shows that it is easy to make something the best it can be but if a challenge is doing it and bring it into the perceivable universe. For that revolutionary idea that you had one day and had to describe to someone, maybe you drew it out yet it never quite matched the image in your mind.

If biologically has taught us anything it is that life is complex at the very least and nothing is simple about it. The same is equal to our understanding if we go back to when it came out your understanding was limited because all the money in research was given to those that thought it had been promised so they focused their assets on seeing the improvement rather than the potential risks. This happened so often that the United States had to set up multiple regulations and organizations to take an intensive look into new products before they are pushed to customers. Everything that has an upside has an equal and opposite downside as Isaac Newtons' 3rd law states, "Every action has an equal and opposite reaction." Most things we use in our lives we see as a positive or a negative thing rather than a balancing item with benefits and drawbacks based on the situation.

Nothing is simple if we dig deep enough and this is the relative ideology of the Dunning Kreuger effect. Which states that there is a point where people no longer care about the effects as long as their prior knowledge was enough for them. That goes into the barrier of intelligence which is a theory that after a certain amount of intelligence people will be more depressed than their intellectually lacking partners just because they see more. People lacking that "space" to acknowledge the full field will be stuck in the good parts because that is how our advertising is built today. In a cycle of how the information is from informing to telling half the story to changing it to be better than what it seems till it is unrecognizable from the source as if the message got sent through a game of telephone. Anything simple is not being looked at by a big enough magnifying glass because in a world of disorder order still is sought and the same can be said for the world of complexity in which simplicity is just a mere sought after quality in the aftermarket world. Most old sayings did not come from anywhere and I suppose there is truth ignorance is bliss, I once wished that I could have anything in the world it would be infinitely and all-seeing wisdom which has its short term upsides but there is no reason to see the unnecessary conflicts of life; somethings are better left as a mystery for one brave soul to stand to up and experience.

We keep trying to make this world equal for everyone when the subconscious bias still exists in everyone's mind. Rather than either adapting to it or changing their views laws have to be made for basic moral human principles. Even though we are all given as "fair" of a chance as possible from birth there are still things that separate us that we cannot have any effect on till we are eighteen and even though we all are given the "same opportunity" we have to separate ourselves to get chosen for our teams. It is interesting how the law strives to make everyone equal yet businesses look for something special, that we constantly get molded by society to fit in.

If I could design the school system and class structure it would be very simple but slightly more time-consuming but due to the ease of a computer, it could be done in probably two programs. The way it should be set up is each teacher that teaches a subject that other teachers are also involved in, generally core subjects, there is a hidden grouping of students for each teacher. Meaning for English 2 Honors, let's say there are 4 teachers, each one is assigned a test score range from last year's final exam. So you would take all the students' scores out of one hundred percent and divide it by the number of teachers, so for this example, each teacher would take twenty-five percent. Thus, teacher A gets the top twenty-five percent of students, teacher B gets from the top twenty-five percent to top fifty percent, teacher C gets from the top fifty percent to the lower twenty-five percent, and finally, teacher D gets the lower twenty five percent to all the leftovers. So then teachers do not need to change their lessons based on how intelligent the class is and it let's most teachers not have to teach multiple classes just because of awkward scheduling or certain accommodations. Note that this would be for classes assigning students to specific classes is more complex than this simple system and it gets more intricate when talking about group seating but I will try to explain my theory.

For assigning students to classes, sort them by grade point average (GPA) highest to lowest for that class. So let us say every teacher has four classes, For teacher A which is the only one I can be bothered to explain before it gets too redundant for me as the writer. So this teacher gets twenty students in a class on that list take them in the order as provided but the period order does not matter: take the with the highest GPA student in that test bracket that the teacher has and put them in seat one, there will be four seats in each table and for this example, there will be five tables. Then take the lowest GPA student of them and sit them in the same group as the "smart" student then for the last two seats take the center students' GPA wise one upper and one lower and sit them in the last remaining. Check the student's schedule for availability for the period and do this system for the next period but only one table and keep doing it so after on the table it switches to the next period till you have it all filled. This would be a great system for a private school since they can control enrollment more so than public schools in most cases. But that in itself does not seem to be too difficult but rather just time-consuming but the part of this that takes heavy processing power is doing this for four core classes which again every teacher has a different level. Making it fairly impossible to do by hand. If someone wants the math for this be my guest it, but you are on your own for that one. For the slower people in the book whenever you increase the possibilities exponentially it does the same thing to processing power and without a quantum computer, this is decryption where we need to try every combination till it just works, which takes way more time than you think.

We can solve problems often with less work then the suffering that comes with it staying around but no one invests in it till it is needed for a personal goal. Because everything is fine and dandy until a rich guy needs it. Because they can change it because why help the common man, they only fuel our society so why do we not treat them that way. There is a fix and that is called socialism because people like the thought of working for your commodities knowing that you are letting someone else not have it. After all, you want it. Promoting competition but if we were to work together as a group of people without nations and differences by race or gender and forget the stupid problems we could be so much farther ahead. To advance further, at least to other worlds we need a nation for Earth and one for every planet like the system that we already have just scaled up. Making federal laws international and those to interplanetary and keep scaling, but that requires a more efficient political system and to that, I do not have the answer but I know someone does, and when that idea comes uptake that person seriously no matter how stupid it sounds or unlikely, support them because it is not like you have a better idea. Build those up that have ideas since they can always be improved but never made worse.

Nothing is perfect but we can all put forth just a little more effort to make it that one step closer and maybe traffic will be that little bit clearer. Every chance starts small and grows and if you do not create the change be an advocate because either we change or something changes us. If it is on our terms it will be easier on society but when mother nature forces a radical change on us out of the blue so many more get hurt because she doesn't care about what happens it just does, it is not going to spare the guys with the biggest bank account. You cannot just bribe a hurricane to avoid your house.

If there is anything these circumstances have taught me, it's that we need to stand together to survive and that mindset should be carried out in business as well as in any other "survival of the fittest" scenarios because together we can move mountains and create companies but alone you can have plenty of thoughts but who will be there to make them a reality. The military has adopted this mindset of survival of the group and not for oneself. They realized that the best way to achieve their goals was through cooperation over competition and a business's vision is no different. It is where it wants to move to and not how much it wants to move. This vision is what should be protected on the survival of CEOs in big houses because sure they did a lot for the company but there are other parts. So why should some get paid and others should not, either way; no one is working so either everyone or no one should be paid. But the cost of paying everyone, someone says in the back, well I know who is getting paid during this time. If everyone kept getting paid then the economy could be kept relatively high as they will still need to buy things and without sacrificing US debt. Currently, one in ten dollars that are collected in taxes is just to pay the interest of the US debt, none of it is even hitting the principle. Companies could most likely have assets for a time like this and others have pandemic insurance, not to mention the fact that they could probably get a better loan than whatever the US government is getting. And a normal paycheck is way better than the stimulus trying to live off of that if you make more than that is going to rough especially if you have a mortgage, and for those who make less than that they are happy till they see the amount in taxes they need to pay on it next year till the national debt of that action is repaid. If it was least reflective of a percent of total income then it would be better but not as good as companies having to pay their employees, but hey what do I know about all this.

It takes ten seconds to grab someone's attention yet we are taught to write essays on relatively unimportant things, for those who want to write their life out yeah that is great but for everyone, don't we think that is a little much. Some tell you to write a good email and immediately think long but what are your thoughts when you receive one? My response is to read the first and last lines to see if I care enough to read the rest as it will probably be unimportant. So you are the cause of this problem and the solution is to grab someone's attention rather than making them grab the air around them.

There is always a sign no matter how subtle or fast there is always a sign and the human brain is good at picking them up in direct interaction when it seems unlikely our brain gives a warning but we tell ourselves it's wrong. You get the feeling the that something is wrong with your school that no one else seems to notice or care about and then you say we are a new rich school nothing could possibly happen, then your parents get an email about what happened and you wonder was I the only won't that noticed, surly not it is a big school after all but no one seemed to care as they were all busy in their own world of selfishness and attention, to look around and realize that today was not a good day to leave your table messy or do something stupid. It just was not the right time. It is also amazing how your brain can tell the difference from serious to an emergency, whether it is a teacher yelling at you or parents telling you to do something you can tell when it means to sink or swim.

To make a better tomorrow we need to look whether it is five years or just five seconds we need to be observant enough to see into the future as a chess player. When the moment eventually comes when you are driving and just wonder how you got where you are, you do not remember even taking the turns to work it just happened. That needs to stop we need to stop idling on autopilot wondering where our time is going, a fair bit of us do this once we get home, whether it is on Youtube or Netflix you put it on and loss from to forty minutes of your life as without even remembering what just happened but when it plays again you feel like you have seen it but cannot quite tell. Sure, you were there but not really while at work. If your days just fly by without or go as slow as a snail without remembering what happened you need a career change as it was not even important enough to remember what happened and how you could care for your clients.

Life is all about giving to get, everything that happens is equal, anything I tell you is equal to what you give me back in return. It is just a quirky thing about our universe. But in average families you wake up, go to school, get a stable degree, and are told to stay in your line till you die. I know you have heard this or have given this advice to your children, wait did I say "advice" I meant to say that you told them this was their only option. Wealthy families tell their kids to try a little bit of everything and to be able to pivot in a moment's notice. So the moment something out of their control happens to just accept it and start on minimizing the loss. The ability to change what you are doing on a moment's notice is a skill that is lacking in society.

I also believe video games can help manifest this skill for those that want it. In RTS games there are random events that are limited only by the length of the game. Meaning that at the beginning of the game you cannot get charged with planetary money laundering and have to deal with those effects, as time goes along more things can happen to you whether it be good or bad but there will be less of them, even though the nuances that they contain can be anywhere from mellow to game-changing. But the early game is all about a lot of simple and small events which compound together, it is the same mechanic used in completely separate ways. But when you get those good events no one restarts but when you roll something unfavorable is when quitting becomes a valid option in your mind. These games are all about strategy, sure in a perfect world two horsemen can take out a musketeer but if said musketeer has the high ground good luck trying. These games are all about rolling with the punches and adapting but if they put the most volatile events at the beginning there would be no reason not to restart. They put them at the end so when you get attached to what you have done you will be less likely to just give up thus improving your skill in that regard.

For those of you that are creating original fiction, whether it be a book, a game, or a realm in art; create a world and not just your product. Even though it will be harder to make a world with reliable and sensible rules it will be worthwhile. Worlds have infinite potential no matter your goal and they can even survive generations. But the easiest way to make a world is with as few mechanics as possible, and to not add new mechanics -if you can help it- compared to expanding upon those that are already there. The reason why worlds are so amazing is that we, constantly, want to escape our own. We do not want to exist in our own skin, but if you turned your life into a show you would still watch it because it cuts out the boring parts. I am thinking about rewriting that original book idea after this just because I would have had more experience. Even when I write now I constantly find it easy to improve and when I stop someone is always there to tell me what to improve but the nice thing is that they do not tell me how to improve, it allows me to still keep my voice yet implement a solution. But do not get me wrong I would be over the moon if someone was like here is a youtube video, watch this and implement it and you are done. But I do think I need to struggle a little more. You know you are doing something new when everyone's solutions do not work for you.

Cost

Point A to Point B,
Zoom Zoom they say,
Many talks about the journey yet have any
actually traveled,
Run along they say,
Go explore,
We walk on supports that only work when
standing still,
Nothing truly stops,
No matter the desire.

Sacrifice or tap out,
Play to win not to float,
You want and I want to fight for it,
They sell a product cheaper then it is,

Read the fine print,
Understand the cost.

Bactria,
The vaccinable part,
First,
We need to learn and understand,
Then solve,
Although our problem forgot the solution.

As if there was a character limit that could
not include it.
There is a lot you can purchase but humanity
is not one,
Most talk about spending as just swipe,
There are unspoken costs not measured.

Back to the original thought about life being
a transaction, everything has a trade-off, and
everything has an effect whether or not it affects
you or if you acknowledge it, it still happens, and
that is the great thing about life; there is no back
button, no reload save, we can not fix our mistakes,
but it is only a mistake from our seat. Perspective is
everything from how we argue, to why there is a
grey area, it's how we look at it. Most people see
youth as an unknowledgeable group of people
when they just lack experience, but they have

different knowledge that's fresh and unchanged by society.

We all see things differently based on the subjective nature of the world itself, and so it values it as subjective, yet we think of it objectively because most of the time we can not negotiate or barter like our ancient ancestors. Since there is no global currency, which determines the price of or benefit of the deal because there is no, the global economy as a whole, unless...

Like a few of you talk, I purposely put everything that comes out of my mouth, there is a reason for it because redundancy hurts, almost as much as my social life. It is okay though being a man of relatively few words unless I have a reason to speak. But that does create some false impressions within life, people in school will think I am smart not saying they are wrong but smart and hard-working are different. I am one of these. Smart because I do not study and take anywhere between two to four AP's in any one year and by smart and amusing society's standard as book smart but by definition rather than by impression if you will. Education is a skyscraper, and I thank my parents for realizing it when I was young, so young in fact, that I do not even remember it. But to further elaborate on my point.

Language, when you first start speaking is a big event that happens when your first word comes out as your first understandable attempt at communication. From there it builds from words to a string of incomprehensible syllables due to one's lack of understanding of language or properties of it. Finally, it escalates to sentences, and sure it does, but this is the point you can have a conversation with them as an equal if you will and with some dubbing down get them to understand. By this time, we are in second to third grade, and we only expand on writing exponentially with thoughts transforming into paragraphs and for most people stopping at papers/essays. As well as slowly fill our heads with more rules of the language that most people never knew or thought about but sometimes followed. This all would have never happened without building on what we already can do, and this same rule applies in transportation, math, and science.

To go with this cycle that I semi setup, we become life forms after we are born that can not move then, we grew and learned to crawl sure some people skip this but then depth perception can be rather flawed when older. After crawling, we learn to stand then eventually walk, but it kind of plateaus after that but in most cases by thirty we have our drivers license, and in most cases we never need to take the test again which I do feel is a little insane with the drivers we have today but what can you do.

Even though this is starting to seem a little redundant, I do need to fill up space so relating to math, and I have created this acronym CASMDES, which means the process of how we learn math till later about high school level because at that point it's not my problem. C for counting the first thing you do, then A for addition for when you first get into real-world situations. I hope you see the trend, S for subtraction the first time we end with a smaller number than when we started. M for multiplication which is the first time we carry a digit more than one to another column and is based on addition. D for **** nope not that, division, ah that seems about right, but this is the first time where we can interact with decimals, fractions, and repeating numbers. E stands for exponents which is the first situation you practically need a calculator to do based on the amount of effort it can to do five to the ninth power it takes extreme brainpower to do it in your head and a fair bit of paper to write it out. The second S stands for square root; this is the point in math where you completely stop trying to do it in your head unless it is perfect, but those are far and few between. I could keep going off on a "tangent", but that is all that is needed for this point.

Science is a subject that never all connects until you reflect on it. This is going to be the point at which I will mostly lose you so. We all are made with cells that eventually build up tissues, then organs, and finally a life form. But to get energy from somewhere for most people something needs to die for you to eat on a day to day basis, just think about that. To fully explain how science connects, you need to look at the base of it all, nothing, and energy.

The truth is we as humans do not know the six questions of our life and if you do not remember elementary school English, it is: who, what, when, where, why, and how. We still basically cannot answer any one of them, and I am going to show you. With who, we know who we are now, speculate on our past, and hope for the future. But we still have no idea who we are relative to the bigger picture as in our role in the solar system or galaxy or even bigger. We also know that we as humans came about from evolution and we also know life came about when the moon struck the Earth; it -apparently- sparked it, not my concern but it did. But we do not know what exists on our planet with creatures still being discovered on the ocean floor that we cannot even imagine based on the environments that they live in, on a day to day basis. So who do we as a society expect anything outside of our current world or our intergalactic role at the point technology is currently? It does not even seem productive to explore or think of those possibilities. Especially when we still have internal wars within our own countries or the fact that we have riots/protests to exhaust our perspectives so that we feel that we are heard. But as we all should be familiar with, we only hear when we have "power" which is and not limited to: money, social influence, importance.

If you ask any kid or adult and ask what we are at our most basic forms, their answer is going to be very simple, cells. But if we know the root and the result, why can we not solve anything in between, if you put it in a mathematical equation, it makes sense. Cells plus X equals sick humans, sure it is oversimplified but isn't that the fun of it, knowing that someone out there is taking offense or pulling out based on a statement you made to make others see your point. But the point is that we are getting just slightly killed by the things on our planets and just as math, responsibilities is a foundation based thing. In most cases your parents never just left you at home for eight hours, most of the time you would either build up to that time or learn the skills required to survive for that long because we all know how it is to resist burning down a house, am I right? But just like building anything, it needs a foundation from which to grow on and expand upon, and we need to be at peace with the fact that we are not ready to explore the external world that we are out of touch with.

Now to when now when means time and now in the universe time means distance so how far are we from the things we need or how far we are...

There is a point before the deadline at which there is no point in actually working on it compared to having faith and let your beliefs match your goals. Granted if you did nothing then you should expect that, but if you honestly put in the work, sweat, effort, or whatever you want to call it results will and there is no shortcut for that. If you try your honest best and put your entire life and soul into it will be seen. The stress you have right before the deadline should be the preemptive celebration for the work you put together and not stressing about the outcome. I do not personally know or believe anything specific but do I know something is out there, yes. Watching everyone and giving them their path that they walk, some fail, some succeed, and others just walked a separate one entirely. This world is not a full internal locus of control and nor is it a full external but a hazy gray combination. Just like an argument in today's society, the solution is a combination of the two sides after all this world is not perfect but it is the one that we were dealt with. So no matter what work you have, do not make excuses, generate reasons on why, and focus on how you can reduce those thoughts "why's." Work for the future, be in the present, and study the past. Time stays the same for businesses and people yet it is used for different things.

Everything you do has to be to build your future because your hero is where you will be in ten years and what you see is your goal and in most cases it is feasible but that goal takes work and it will not happen overnight. When forming a good habit make sure you do it every day then focus on the time and the quality. But for that time that you set for yourself to do this work make sure it is spent on it and not on anything else, consider it as a date. During which you should not be on your phone nor talking to others more attentively then your guest. But get into an environment where you can do something like a specific spot in your house for that work, whether it is an extraocular hobby or job, create a space for it to live in your life away from everything else. So if you are thinking about going back to college to get or finish your degree. Create a certain spot only for it and it cannot be your desk where you do all your other work or your bed where you sleep. Someplace special for your mind and a separate room works best so as you enter the space you are priming your brain to those thoughts as you enter the room. Allowing for it to know its goal before it gets there because you have no other reason to go in there, and if you were to choose a space where you do other things it distracts your subconscious and your brain sometimes cannot identify the proper purpose of your being in that space. Such as a college student who studies on their bed, they are so sleep deprived that their brain wants them to sleep yet they have an important test tomorrow that they must study for and in a short micro sleep you forget about your studying and your subconscious takes over and you fall asleep. Then the panic sets in for the morning as they frantically study for their goal which was to pass, they tried cramming the night before and that was overruled by their bodies needs because that "space" has multiple purposes, then they want to get a good score so before they cram yet it is too late to affect the outcome and so that image that they say of themselves was in their mind but it could not stand the test of reality due to excess stress and procrastination. If that did not do it for you how about in your computer, every part of it has a separate function or even the human body you find cells specific to the organ in the organ and not anywhere else, normally you do not see heart cells in the liver. Even your brain has different areas depending on the information that needs to be processed, people say you only use ten percent or whatever number they use but that is only at one point, in your house you do not actively use every room at one point in time. But if you look at its usage throughout the day or even a week you will see that every room has a purpose.

We are paid in two ways: the one that society expects, money, and the second one which should be chased but is often forgotten and that is experience. We should be paid in both but often when we are young we are told to learn over a paycheck because internships are more valuable but that short term monetary gain if saved and accounted for all other factors involved will equate to the same value as the internships since it will cost the same time. Many will not agree with this but if fully broken down it does make sense and work if all factors are accounted for where there are endless amounts no matter how small. But those people that say the internship is better, why does that perspective change over time, it really should not but people are hypocrites and sure you will need more money as you age into adulthood. So my rule of thumb is that when getting into a field to get an internship and after you are in the door go for a job as in reality this is the most efficient way. This process would be repeated plenty of times throughout your career as you gain two things from that job which are again money and experience. Once your job stops giving you experience there is no reason to stay as you are no longer learning.

Ultimately when you are stuck at a crossroads and the decision seems so hard but in reality, in the grand scheme of things both are equal even though they have separate consequences it does technically balance and the good are just subjective to you and as society's standards as a whole. I would give examples but I believe you get what I am talking about. When learning under someone who does not learn their day job learn the specialty within the job. Let's say you have an apprenticeship with a mechanic, do not learn how to be a mechanic but learn how to build a good clientele if that is your teacher's specialty, do not waste the opportunity just because you want to learn something else or go abroad. The master is that way for a reason and even if it seems useless at the moment it will come in handy either directly or indirectly. If you are studying under a businessman that made a shell company learn that part, the unique part about everyone is the most important part you need to learn because for some reason it does not work out you can learn business anywhere but not "their business."

We encourage people to take risks but when we have to, we say it is too risky. They tell you to take risks but the ones you want to everyone say no or you do. We are told to take risks in a place that was created in a zero-risk environment.

People can self reflect but a system projects its self-reflection on to others. Jobs say they want risk-takers but make sure they have experience because they do not want to risk hiring a clueless person. It is all just a beautiful hypocrisy.

The test of time, we build systems and things to last forever yet there is no reason to as it will never get there and if it does discoveries will be made to make it obsolete. I ask people about certain systems and the only ones they believe needed to be fixed are the ones that do not help them and the ones they do not have confidence in. I believe in the near future we will need either a new type of currency or a new economic system and I think it is going to happen in Africa which is the global economic battlefield for companies. But then again what do I know I am only sixteen, young, naive, and most importantly sober. According to a majority of people, I should sit quietly rather than ask questions and it is mainly based on mindset some people say to their kids their doctor is just trying to do his job site and follow directions and other who say the doctor is you friend that has studied a lot to help inform kids like you about your body. In the second scenario, kids are more likely to speak up and ask a question that has been on their mind or tell their hair barber that they are hurting them. And it is all set by the parent and their choice of language which was created based on their mindset. Even though they are associated with socioeconomic status this is not limited to the people that bleed green. We set the president for our lives with some of the smallest things.

The price tag of something is the attempted objective value of something that has subjective value. So when the price is low enough, the objective value is equal to or lower than your subjective value leading to it being okay I'll buy it or to this is a steal. The only way that we trade items is with currency and most of it does not have any value apart from the confidence that people put into it. If everyone did not believe in the dollar, no matter how much you had it would be worthless and the same thing goes for other concepts like the stock market. If everyone lost faith in a company or the entire system it would fail, much like banks.

It is all based on false confidence, that type you show off at a bar when you see a beautiful girl. If your greatest fear was between you and that girl you would gladly pretend like it was not there and bask in the happiness until it came time for you to deal with that fear rather than going around it. At that point, you only have two options to end your fear or your relationship. If you end the relationship the system crumbles but if you fight the fear there will always be another one, but together you fight it and learn from it forgetting about the people that work in the past as you live in the present. This long analogy is to show that if we keep believing in the system and those running it believe it, it can still exist but always be challenged and improved. But if we listen to those financial analysts they look at what was possible, not what is, and just because you look with yours does not mean that they are not missing something. The answer might only seem to be infrared. I know it takes a lot to trust in a system these days especially with all countries that did go downhill based on only a couple peoples actions and as naive as it sounds it truly seems that we will need to believe in power as if we were living in a Disney movie as silly as that sounds.

In an economy money needs to be recycled and with these current predicament kids like me are experiencing going through this with our parents and we are just old enough to feel the financial strain but not quite old enough to help and that is going to lead to a lot of changes when we end up being our parent's age or even younger as this event came out of the blue and with today's mindset of paying it tomorrow will not be out thought process. We saw what it did to our parents, our friends, and our family. And even though this came out of the blue and no one could predict its effects, the mindset of tomorrow only works if tomorrow was the same as today. When we think ahead we do not plan for everything, we take our current feelings and project them into the future reflecting the quality of tomorrow based on the feelings of today.

This generation will learn to save but I am not sure if we will learn much more than that. You can have ten thousand dollars in a savings account if something happens but every year that it sits there it loses value, in most cases. In today's world inflation is greater than interest, so when I was a true child the pitch of banks was sold to me and I believed it but in reality investing is the new savings, and with all the potential investing could lead to lower interest loans. I am not talking about a house or a car even though in the next five years the interest of houses is going to be at its lowest. What I am talking about is loans for companies. We have a good chance of turning into the people to pay upfront for everything we own, and truly take control of the money we have going in and that's great. But that was all speculation on my part I believe it will happen but really who knows, what this event will cost us long term. What I can say is that I am glad for this to have happened now compared to any other time in history.

The best people see value differently from the money it is worth but how it affects them and the world around them, they account for costs like a general on a battlefield. When you have the wrong set of eyes you only see the price tag. People ask me what gives me the right to write this book about how we live when you have not even finished high school. They ask me for my credentials and I say I have been observing the system for sixteen years while you have been living it, unable to take a step and sure you might have a college degree or know what it feels like to not have money, but I do not, just because I am a child? Because I did not get certified as an all-nighter I know nothing, or is it the risk factor?

Time

Walk,
Run,
Fly...
The time is passing by,
The endless cycle runs,
Endless we see,
But purpose we feel,
When one and zero are both equally
pointless,
In a gigantic void filled with yourself,
Yet we experience day and night,
One never different from the next.

Events through life are the achievements,
To keep the game going,
Running on the hamster wheel,
With a different cage,
All the furniture is just to obscure reality,
Reality is the worst thing known,
Cannot be changed nor begged,
Just is,

We live in a sandbox yet we breathe life,
Those who set the terms of life's contract
added a loophole,
Signing is optional,
Not matter if it looks forced,
This how life got separated from reality,

Time,
Changed and morphed,
Never the same;
Creating it own plain,
Only to be seen later.

As technology improves sending messages takes less and less effort but does that mean we should employ these methods because most do not see the downside of sending an email or a text message rather than talking with the person or calling them. People can tell when you put effort into something and they can also sense it in your communication method. If you take time out of your oh so busy day to talk with them about an issue or to acknowledge their feelings. They will feel valued and important, and whether they actually are is a different story. Someone said it best, "You are not what you think you are, you are not what others think you are but you are what you think others think you are."

The question of what I contribute to my community is a question that I will not only be answering now, but one that will be asked throughout my life, and there is no reason to sugar coat it, so the simple answer is nothing at all. I do not go out of my way to help, but at the same time, I still do it, but at the same time, I do not consider my community when making decisions since it is always going to be there or there will be another to take its place. Especially since it does not give me a reason to, sure it is not a bad one but does average or just above average quality for praise. The average student does not get praised for their grades since the honor roll starts with all A's and B's with no C's, as far as I know, C's are considered average. Based on how this system should work is that the community makes the tenets feel as if they should give back because of how much they care about the status of these tenets. So until I have a reason to help my current community, I will change nothing about myself to accommodate. However, these are just my beliefs based on how leadership works and essential priority management. There also seems as if there are little measurable gains from spending time this way other than dopamine, which you could get from a lot of different ways in which properly are more efficient. Helping my community is especially beneficial to me based on my age and the value of community service hours in high school. When I do decide to help out, I make a choice not to accept these hours as payment or compensation since when I help people out, it is out of the goodness of my heart, nothing more or nothing less. No matter what my guidance counselor says/advises, it is still my life, and my choice might as well make use of this power while I still have it. Sometimes just sometimes, the minority makes a better decision.

When we truly want something we will work for it and the thoughts inside your head will turn from, "I cannot afford this" to "How can I get this." And when you have a drive you go from when we can stop it hurts to I can't get back up anymore I can't feel my body. One is an excuse and the other is a reason. Once I got that in my head I went from stopping fairly quickly to have "godly" amounts of energy and just general efficiency for the task that II and many others never thought was possible.

To get out of bed we need a reason, life in itself is meaningless and so is death, but just because it is that does not make living worthless. We are the leaders of our house because without us there would not exist "our house", it would be different just because we are not there. Visionaries are the ones that separate Apple from Microsoft, they give it an identity and a tomorrow, yet the people of today working and helping just support it for a tomorrow are inherently worthless. Every tooth in a gear needs to be the same size for it to turn although companies are already lopsided by this ladder-like thinking as if going higher allows for a wider ladder yet it just gives a greater vision. But everyone has a place in the ladder so why do some get paid more for an arguably equally vital job. Time can be used to describe the ladder: the past, present, and future. The past is the customers. They reflect what work they were able to do in the past and how successful they were based on that work and it allows for today to happen. Even though this part of marketing is underestimated the ones that achieve mastery of this, mastery of free marketing, normally products that outperform the expectations of everyone are the ones that spread naturally. Just off the top of my head is Minecraft with the original creators and Tesla. They forged their present and most likely sealed their future, but this requires quality as one of the ingredients of their products. Just like when people find a good deal when they find a good product is nothing different; it still releases that same flood of dopamine. I do not know about you just I trust my friends and family a lot more than any shady ad about feeling and how much you need this in your life as if it will be your second heart; looking at you Apple.

There is no true value of people in companies as of now, it is lost, and I believe that it is going to be a while before it is found. For the sake of everyone reading common people will be referring to any and everyone, the customer interacts with from the time they enter to when they exit. Leaving all the "behind the scenes" and upper management to dealing and preparing the company for its future. The apparent common people allow it to continue its day to day tasks and to exist to make it to its future. It is vital to make a customer want to come back and to have employees that want to be there, that should be obvious but doing that is often a lot harder. My solution to this consists of three steps: observation, reasoning, and action.

If you remember anything from physics every reaction has an equal and opposite reaction, which is Isaac Newton's Third Law of Motion. So when an employee or group of, are not performing their best or do not have the desired attitude then ask them. Then with the feedback, try to improve or fix it even if it means a higher wage or something that adds cost to you because trust is valuable so you need to treat it that way, take a page from the mafia or other such gangs. A couple of things are needed to be kept in mind for a system like this to work such as abuse of the system and an open atmosphere. The employees need to be able to talk with someone with more power than themselves without feeling obligated to respond in a certain way. No pressure is the best for when you want the truth and even if they are not their best because of personal reasons try to make their day better or propose a solution to make them happier. But what needs to also be implemented is some sort of a system to ensure that you are not being exploited for your generous resources, whether it is an employee that reports for promised benefits. But the purpose of this is not to punish but rather to build everyone up. Another solution could be what Henry Ford did to prevent unions which were to hire people to "accidentally " change their views the good old fashion way. But of course, this method would need to be modernized and not violent to be legal yet I still think learning from gangs will reap plentiful benefits, being the business of trust and cash.

The next step requires you to weigh out the "value" of the establishment in question relative to the company and competitors as we all should know by now one man's trash is another man's treasure. But in value I am not talking purely numbers but including sentimental value, nor does this need to be done on an accrual basis. No calculator is needed but general knowledge or revenue versus expenses is needed. I believe that the reasons young people do not stay in their jobs for long are because there are no long term benefits and that there is no loyalty. These days if your store or company does not make a certain mark it must be because there are too many people and so they lay them off but they could send that in training them to be better at what they do. But you need to decide if some cash (relatively) is worth an entire employee; the worst thing is the value at which human life is held yet companies might lay someone off not knowing their situation and kill them without even knowing. Does the company go to jail, no, does anyone, no. But their lives do not lose value so is an exploit; nature has no exploits yet everything we touch does. Maybe we should take a hint, that system just did not work rather than let us try to fix it. Even though that is a good mindset, it might not be the best use of time and or resources. But the main point is that you need to be able to visualize value and sometimes profit off of it. What I mean by this is hiring convicts that say and proved that they have changed might have some unseen benefits. As they could have to learn a lot in the big house that most would not realize in the free world.

Time for the hardest part, taking action, whatever your gut feeling turns out to go with it, especially in cases that involve human interaction. When talking everyone's body displays words you can either pick up on or your gut does on its own. They can speak anything but they may show something completely different from the words they do not say. Sometimes it is okay to go with how you feel rather than the number on your calculator especially as we move to a more technologically advanced society. Show them their growth at given time intervals, show them how they have grown. Whether it is knowledge or sales but make sure they see their future with you, not for you. Most of us want to make a difference and make us feel like we are. Some days if you see us say "hey you are doing a great job, keep it up" or something like that to give them emotional backing. Do not lie to them, they will know and no one likes a liar. You want them to work with you, not for you, often the ones in the front lines see the best way to attack, not the commander safe at his house. Let them offer advice and suggestions even if they are ideas that are poorly formed, they can be based for you to help turn them into a reality.

But the people at your company that make up its future are the researchers and inventors. They are creating and designing the products you will be selling to your future clients and when you undercut the future, it eventually comes back and hits with a vengeance whether it is lack of business, lower school ranking, or a preventable disease becoming a pandemic cost-cutting from future-proofing never ends well and if you still do not believe me look at the New York City transportation system, especially the subways. All rusty and such because they used that which was supposed to go to repairs on something else because we do not need to repair it now so tomorrow and now it is tomorrow and it is now beyond repair with an exquisite amount of money they definitely do not have now. So if you can afford to keep them, let them stay as they control the amount of time you get to be open and you should reward them as such.

When something happens, it can be very important to its success. Now you will never truly know a perfect time but for a logical person like me; it is just a feeling. Like when you enter the state of flow and the adrenaline starts pumping. You feel like a fight scene is about to burst out in front of you, whether it is something as boring as selling stocks at a really good price or clutching a game win in a video game, the feeling still happens.

But when we are too impatient to wait for that time we might end up throwing all our hard work away, in an instant. Even if the logical choice is against your gut like the statistics do not support it or it is just a straight-up crazy jump into that deep end. On a race track, you can only get ahead by taking risks because assuming all your competitors drop out is just about impossible, that being said defense is a viable strategy assuming there is a reason behind it. Back to the track metaphor, if there is a corner coming up that you see and realize your opponent will not have enough time to stop, play safer and risk miss guessing their limits compared to following as that will end up with you going the wrong way. That voice in your head has had thousands of years of "experience" even though it might not be directly translatable. Imagine something like Tesla was formed a year or earlier, most likely it would have been too soon and it would have failed based on the lack of viable clients that were willing to buy an electric car after whatever car company in the 90s tried to make one that ended up looking like a spaceship. Or if it was formed later a company like Zero Motorcycles might have expanded into the car industry and have capitalized on the lack of competition. Yes, those are all possible scenarios in another universe, which does appear to be true at least theoretically, but that did not happen so I could spend more time in the what-if's but at the same time it does not matter but I believe you got the message.

Let me set this up as some Youtube clickbait, please do not demonetize me for this, "Your Reality Doesn't Matter." The reason why I saw that is that you are the only one in your shoes and no one else can one hundred percent see your perspective of things no matter how hard they try. They are not with you and your thoughts one hundred percent of the time so they can offer advice but you need to sit at a table with yourself and see if it applies to you, what they see is very different then reality in most cases. On the outside, they could see a happy family of four with one child that has the tendencies of a delinquent and say to throw him in therapy because that works and it helped their friend or family member and how they used to be so much worse but you only see them for like fifteen minutes a day. But the real reason he is like that is that he sees all the financial pressure you are under and cannot positively exert that energy, and when you leave the house you become one of those depression commercials where you can have your handy smile on a stick and keep walking and everyone sees that. No one sees the problem, but no matter how hard you try to hide a problem there is no way to do it in a full proof manner. There will always be evidence but does anyone pick the evidence up and evaluate it or talk themselves out of it. That way you present yourself is how the world sees you, if you are an influencer and you take all these photos with smiles and rainbows that is what your audience will believe, after one corner of a beat-up car in frame with a bunch of hypercars, could not possibly be hers. Until someone looks into it and searches up police reports or some psychopathic tracking and finds out it is them, but it requires a certain type of person to think about how it is they decided to do research.

A lot of us will just take facts at face value without contention if in a group situation or if it seems believable enough but all we need to do is talk to our phone and there is the answer. That method is an easy way to spread misinformation or to hustle someone, an even better way to do some especially if you are on the younger side, say your parent or grandparent told you this as this adds credibility since these people have lived longer and in our society means they have more knowledge with their experience. Not to mention the type of person that is needed to openly contest people when saying it at the moment, takes a lot because you indirectly claim to have more knowledge then someone older than you, and that is already an uphill battle, then what if you are wrong. Is that possible embarrassment worth correcting this person, worst comes to the worst for the person spreading this information the person he was trying to convince will just say, yeah, sure, bud, in his head and continue with their day and you will be able to just move on to your next target? As opposed to without this knowledge would lead to a public confrontation where you will need to admit that they are right before someone pulls out the old Google and there will not be another target in at least a five hundred meter range.

The fair majority of people will believe anything assuming it is reasonable allowing it to be chalked up as a bad day when in reality it is an issue. The way people see you can very easily change how people view you, and most of that judgment is done in ten seconds, you do not even need to open your mouth and people will already have chosen a side, so in reality, you do not need to be what need for your effect, you just need to appear to be what you need for your effect. After all, those burn fat workouts with the before and after photos still get people to join them by showing health issues on the left to Mr. or Mrs. Sexy on the right not realizing that it was either extreme photoshop mixed with not eating or a massive mid-life crisis life the doctor walking in like I'm surprised you are not already dead with the stuff you shove down there. It just tripping the right cord of, I could have been over already, I do not what to be over so they get the fight or flight experience for losing weight, and in most cases, you do not have the desire that hand-picked person has, after all, if you did you would figure it out without a program.

There is something the world of PC gaming (also known as a personal computer, I know I taught someone that today) taught me and that was the number of indie games out there. For those of you that are slightly confused; it means the amount of basically freelance developers that were making their great games without huge teams of people. It showed me that as much as there is a mass-market there is also a niche one but it may not be on your terms. It opened my eyes to see all the possibilities that are not ads from the big companies of that industry, and that if you look hard enough in any market there is always a small underdog and that options are everywhere if I open my mind and search not with my eyes but glasses. I gained sight with this, and if you never needed glasses what I mean is that before you know you need glasses you most likely thought this was as clear as the world is, with the gradual changes slowing getting worse, unless it gets tested. Like you used to be able to see the board at the beginning of the year but know you cannot, in most cases you chalk it up to being closer even though you have had the same seat all year. But when you finally get that eye test and see what true clarity is, your world expands like when you learned to walk.

People say to be resourceful and to use everything available to you but they do not mean that. My parents say to work smart rather than harder so I do, and if they as I tell them how, it's not like they can do anything about it, I am just following what they preach, and isn't that what any Father would want? So why is cheating such a bad thing, when everyone agrees to cheat it is called cooperation, so if I spent my time in a school set up in a social system where every kid would only need one in every five assignments. It is still going strong and for the sustainability of it, I cannot tell you the steps here but feel free, to guess. A hint is that it is simple with multiple nuances in place. They say I need to know this information for the future which I will truly know the answer to that when I am dead but assuming nothing on the internet disappears like a nude picture shouldn't using google are apps that give you the answer be a fair game after it's not like things disappear and it does not seem like an internet connection is going to be a rarity in the future. Maybe it is to learn they tell you not to use it but I say that you can learn more by thinking outside the box rather than flipping to a textbook because hopefully in your craft you will be better than any textbook and when you run into an issue what are you going to do. When you search up answers you will learn to skim, and maybe learn a random piece of information along the way if you see anything interesting. If it was really important to you, you would have intrinsic motivation and learn it without anyone telling you to. But why is it that people get mad when you find an exception in their states such as people using the words everyone and all, and you abuse their word choice to destroy their argument, it is not your fault that they chose those words nor is it your fault for making it appear as it was simply untrue. And for a solid fact, there is no way the definition of the word was your fault so use it against them, as the point is only as strong as its weakest support. So when we become resourceful and look for that vulnerability why do people say get mad at us for it. They should have spent more time formulating it and take a page out of most great speakers and stop and think before you respond. I could only imagine if 911 was as fast as people trying to counter an argument, they would be there faster but are the police going to stop a fire? Let's just say you do not like the silence while you think, make like a salesman and dodge till you can counter, think of arguing as a game where as long as you are not taking damage you are winning, and that's not wrong. When you dodge their attacks they will get frustrated and create openings for you to strike but do it, when you know you can win not just when you can.

Silence

All this noise,
All of it,
Just fake,
All the things that take time,
Filling up peoples lives with air,
As they try to make it look like an atmosphere,
All the chemicals wanted but few have facades,
Ding,
Chirp,
Vvv...

All self-made noise,
But when real noise happens,

The boy calls wolf once again,
Till he sinks and wonders why he could not swim,
Living on an ocean but he never asked to,
But other noises stopped his living.

No...
No...
No...
Yes may not be the savior we want but the one we need,
Resistance it the only method of growth,
Say yes for one minute,
He,
Needed a yes,
Though he was too stubborn,
The negative thoughts seeped into action.

Education is a business, even those that claim to be non-profits still need to be vaguely in the black or around it at the very least. But when the non-profit acts like a successful for-profit business, there is a clear problem. It will not affect the executives that are paid very handsomely, but it will affect society as a whole when these young minds can have power. Since we are always behind in the problems we solve, whether it be generational issues or problems being created today, we always react after the fact. Look at Los

Angeles. It used to have smog, but when it was building up, no one cared, but once it got out of hand is when we started to correct it, and now it is one of the cleanest air cities in the world. The College Board currently holds a monopoly over education since there needs to be a national standard to which students are held to predict performance for college since grades are so inaccurate since it is based on the school. They can even vary significantly based on the teacher having less school, so this is needed. But why is there only one, and why does the government not consider it a monopoly? The reason it is not a monopoly is that it is a non-profit, so it should not because it is not supposed to make a profit, but that is far from reality. It charges about eighty dollars for every ap test and similar prices for each SAT and ACT. Sometimes schools will cover the cost, but that is only when you pass for many, with each ap test having about a fifty percent pass rate nationally.

But as said earlier, they are the only national standard that is recognized by just about every school. Each test is curved based on the relative difficulty but not comparable to the students, and this human resources and computational power does take much energy, so it would be unlikely for any other organization to get into it. However, the competition it will create will have exponential benefits to consumers and schools around the globe. With this monopoly, education is limited to what they choose to test you on further, shoving down real-world use, examples, or even subjects. They control training, and that is controlled by the government, which is the main thing limiting our education. Teachers are not allowed to teach every subject, they are not allowed to inform students about money properly and what they do educate is old and vetted strategies to not get the most out of your money. The rich do not want more of themselves.

Ever since computers have taken over calculations, most errors were caused because of the human behind the tool and not the tool itself. Systems are made to reduce, but every so often, it fails, and havoc appears as if a random boss you did not realize you had to fight. Sometimes the best way to learn is from others, but maybe not in the same way that you think we can all learn from each other and build, but what about learning from other's mistakes? There was a time when I was a little younger and a little more immature when I decided to cut one out of my life, and I felt the need to justify it to everyone to prove that it needed to happen. But today, I found out how artificial that was and how it was supposed to happen naturally. Sure enough, the same thing that I did to this kid occurred and happened to me, so I decided to be calm first and evaluate the situation first, then about my emotions and then finally about my decision. No matter how I wanted to act at that moment, it would not change anything about the situation I am still in nonetheless. So I became productive to account for this, and when everything seemed like it was falling apart, I thought about if I put others in place before and sure enough I had, but it was not this bad. So I apologized to him and wanted him to know that if he needed something I would be there for him but nothing more. But I would not have realized this if it were not for the situation I was put in and some would say that karma and others bad luck; but I am here no matter the cause and need to get through it, at least I learned from it and applied it to help someone else. Right now, I do believe that it is a bit of both a terrible mix of bad luck and karma, but there is no more of a reason to complain after all someone is always going through worse no matter how much this does annoy me.

The most important things we sometimes cannot admit to ourselves, takes having someone else point it out for true clarity to begin. This is the overall reason why I wrote this book to help others and to help my future self. When I am in a situation where I need advice and my mind is drawing a blank, I will have a place to refer to for my best and thoughtful self, unhindered by the emotion by the current emotion. People do not write books for money, at least successful ones do not, they write to tell a story, and yeah I could do that but at the same time... that would require an interesting life; I am just going to stick to my idioms and minuscule personal analogies. But back to what I was saying, bias, especially in people (emotions), can lead down an undesired path of regret, since your heart fuels you but your mind guides you. No matter what you need both and you need to make sure you keep both in check since your heart is the end goal and what gets you up in the morning that is past money, it is far deeper than that. Your mind is the rational side of yourself that is there for your survival and as a safety net also like the checks in balances system within oneself. If both clear the thought and idea it is safe to go off and do, but when both bodies do not agree more times than not you are going to need a "neutral" third party to evaluate whether you should or should not legislate your idea into your life. Its battle is not the only one, but it is one of the more complex ones; some others that will be included are the battles or long term and short term and how thoughts mindsets should be able to be swapped like gears in a manual. The people around you will always want to help but they only can admit that you need it and ask, not a whisper but yell it loud from the rooftops and many will come far and wide; they need to be able to hear it. It is not the number of calls you make but the loudness at which your voice quakes. Understand that your first option in most cases is not the right one, it often appears with great speed to get you to sign the paper, and it normally appears to make the process quick and easy, they will use speed to hide its flaws but with the proper research which they do not want you to do can very easily make your life a whole lot better in the long run.

We stand up to spark change or react to it, but did we ever sit and look at why it is happening and maybe let it, because there is a reason why it is happening which we investigate and there is also a purpose which is what it serves to accomplish and in most cases pretty open to speculation but it is how you look at it. Let's just take this Corona thing the purpose technically is to spread, but its actual purpose to us could be not to underestimate diseases or it could have served as a warning for overpopulation mixed with too much carbon, and it would serve to help fix some of these problems without technology. Is anyone mentioning what out of the box things we could learn from this, even if they are not directly related? I believe our society is a little too short-sided overall because as we should all know by now is that every reaction has an equal opposite response so when we do new things and are unaware of the consequences are we going to do it in moderation or are going to say full send because it is the new oil even though we do not know its full or nominal amount of our actions. Especially because the population on our planet is expected to keep growing so one new power source for maybe about ten billion people and extra power draw because that is how technology appears to be going. Suddenly the effects of carbon that we have now will happen faster and most likely be harder to stop, but even though we have surprisingly good regulations all you need is one person to not do their job and that is it.

I am at the point in my life where I am starting to look at careers and so are my friends and they will recommend a job to be and state the amount of amount money it makes per year based on a median standard and I sit here wondering why that median number matters because I know the job at the very least pays for a house or else it would not be a career field so that is out of the way, I know I am not going to be average at what I do, I know I will try to be the best knowing myself and I know that whatever I want I will figure out how to afford, even though this is naive if I go where the money is there will not be any more left once I get there and on top of that I will also not enjoy it. I rather enjoy one-third of my life and life on a futon then waste a third of my life doing what everyone else is, and that is working for the man, and where he wants you to be. I know there are tons of other people out there that know computer science is a booming industry and that is great for those that have felt they tried ever stand a career and this is what they needed but that is not for me. I do know who to code and I even do it in my spare time if I want to make a program to do certain functions I am too lazy to do. But all it takes is one lazy person slash employer that creates a program to take a language in and automatically write it into code and put it into a "lower-level language." Then the barrier to entry is going to be lower causing for there to be a greater supply than demand which causes the amount of money each person gets paid to go down especially if they are not good at it, thus making it less desirable. On top of that, why would an employer now hire people that know how to code compared to those that have ideas? It seems that I am the only person that sees it this way so I'll keep my theory silent and see if it comes through if it does all I am going to hear is why did you not say anything. If life was more spontaneous or education was faster to get I could see the good with the flow mindset for work. Like analyze what the world needs now and study it as that will be a jackpot especially if I realize it before most do, but education takes a fair amount of time, and hopefully Corona will not be around for that much longer, causing a major in fabrication to not be in demand anymore unless you get lucky with some random events. I recommend my friend's career for things they have interest in and they are like well that does not make as much money, and I'm like once you pay taxes it is all the same because you will be forced in a different bracket anyways. And everyone should know that you have to stay at the top of each bracket but not go over it to keep the most amount of money on top of that you also need to be smart with your income. Just like working out if you focus all your energy into eating less and never touching a weight in most cases will leave you disappointed much like if you focus all on income without considering lowering expenses.

Not to mention the stigma with my generation with debt, because I tell people I expect to have debt by the time I am thirty and the stop focusing and cut me off, say things like, why would want that or other such close-minded things, and I told them when you need answers from a friend at that moment but you had nothing to give you, you said they owe me one, and how many times have you done that without a second thought when it benefited you at the moment. Or about the fact that debt is good and bad, depending on what you spend it on, relative to assets. As everything is balanced if you look on every spectrum, which is just about impossible but if we ever become a hive mind or gestalt consciousness you might understand. And what do those do when they get into an argument like one says get out of my head and the other is like it was hurting anyway. Just some shower thoughts, but back to the topic at hand, if you take a loan on a sports car no it is not going to look good for you assets unless you race it and receive money with it or you keep it long enough to where it becomes valuable because of its rarity. The cup is still half whether it is empty or full but the real question is, was it being filled or drunk because you still have the same debt but does it work for you, or do you work for it.

In your newfound ability to be quiet and be more logical and remember odd things that show you care, the reality is up to you but if you remember something that they have only said once or have insinuated too without saying it, you appear to be better than before. Watch for everyone's perspective, like if you are about to sit at a roundtable you should already have talked with them and found either a weakness or their purpose in being there, by simply asking open-ended questions that seem out of aimlessness and curiosity. Simple things like, "Hey, what do you do for fun?" or "Are you new here?" Just to get them talking about themselves because no one thinks that the debate begins till everyone sits down and it starts once you guys walk it, it is all mind games from thereon. No one is going to answer those questions in such a short manner that you cannot ask a follow-up question and no one is going to refuse it after people do a lot to avoid awkwardness and that is one of the many lengths they will go. Silence in itself is a mind game, causing them to talk more but it can be used for over-analysis, not to mention turning people against each other. Like if someone goes fishing for the information you just lie to them, after all, they do not know. I took this one from women who do not give their real numbers to men. But if they do not know you, they cannot fact check you unless you have something on the internet that says otherwise or there are others there that can blow your position. What I mean by this is suppose you make a post that says your favorite color is green and then you say to them in your face that your favorite color is red, that bring a red flag in their head and tells them not to trust you, but if they acknowledge and try to call you out would say it has been a long time things have changed or some form of a smokescreen but if they do not confront you that is where paranoia can enter based on the silence. If someone is going to ask about you to someone else they will tell the truth and that is your lie decor unless you make them look like the bad guy and do some gang sign to tell them to hit and be the bad guy. It is just a giant game of chess with some underrated strategies. I will not state all of them but every strategy can work if played properly, but adapting is the other half.

Logistics, the thing that allows for your shirt to fly more miles then you in your life, obviously including all the parts, for those of us that have been graced to play games with logistical management we should know there is no such thing as winning but how will I lose, or efficiently. As we should know is that there will never be a system with one hundred percent efficiency, no matter how close it gets, kinda like hand sanitizer which will never kill all germs. Logistics is the game that never ends, demand will always change and there will always be news no matter how boring a society, that's assuming we are all still human. If we had a robotic empire it would be easier and more reliable to transport items but there are still planetary events like tornados or interplanetary events like solar flares and such so it would feel easier and more reliably till relative time accelerates once again. What I mean by this is the theory that we will never be able to live long enough, for exam generation A have an average lifespan of fifty years, then during generation B and their life there find a way to live longer till about seventy and they are happy but generation C is like we still live so short so once they have all fallen off generation D finds a way to live longer than expected and they are happy. So the perpetual cycles of life span is proven with human history, but not one hundred percent confirmed but it does make sense. Overall we are not grateful for what we have and are often sad about it until it decreases then we show gratitude or when it gets unexpectedly bigger because it was now what you signed up for.

The psychopaths and stalkers of the world are normally the quiet ones at the back of the class. Even though you can get a lot of information from just the internet these days, they learn a fair amount of information just from the conversations they have with others as they slowly start to piece everything together. For the most part, people do not pay that much attention to their surroundings to tell when they are being there as long as you appear to have a reason to be there. Again people do not like being awkward so they most likely will not confront you unless you look like a someone sketchy or harmful and in most cases, the psychopaths do not really have a feeling that they give off and just exist and that for some reason does not trigger a red flag in someones but instead allows them to blend in. They say eyes are the windows to the soul and that is true, just by looking at the eyes and general area around them, but not the mouth you can see intent. You can fake a smile pretty well, all you have to do is think something happy but it is very hard to tell your eyes to smile.

Mismatched body language is a problem, it means something is wrong but it will not be obvious so you just gotta keep an eye out like how you should be driving, but people often forget to look left when making a right on a stop sign since they are the only people on a public road. The best way to practice lying with people you know is, to lose some battles, what I mean by this is to create a tell that you can control so they know when you are lying and your tell, which you should work to minimize. So you will sometimes lie about common things, then you wait for a second then do your tell to show them you are lying but in reality that makes them feel better because it was small and the fact they called you out on it. But then slowly start fading out your tell that you created and you will watch you get away with it. If their body language picks up that it is a lie, do tell you created and take the hit. Let's say that it is too late to do your tell, then chalk it up to a communication error like you did not hear them right to say that you did not know even if it is a lie because as long as you do not play that card too often then you will think it is for real. I am not saying this for harmful intent but for someone to reverse engineer it to create a counter-strategy. After all, the only things that make a game fun are difficulty and the randomness it creates.

I am a fan of doing things on my own schedule and if it aligns with someone else's yay. I am this way because my schedule is different from the generic nine to five. I have most of my brain-power from 9 pm-3 am this is the time when I can blitz through work and activities but when it is out of that range it is basically me stalling till that time and then it gets done fast. This is my time, you find yours because that will be the time to work on your future or side hustle, for the most part, everyone goes to school or work, and if you are not where you want to use this time to catch up. Work and school should you cruising in sixth gear down the highway, just chill even though it is harder than idling, but during that prime time you are just shifting to get the best time, and after your time you can just look back and see all the work you have done and be proud of it as that time could very much be an entire days work if not more.

Unfortunately, this is where you cross the stage of graduation, leave here, with the knowledge, more like random facts I bestowed upon you. I hope you have enjoyed your flight and please be sure to re-read this again when the time is right (and send the money). This feels a lot like high school, you could have missed it and been okay but because you have it, it can rework your entire life. That is if you trust a sixteen-year-old, and just to potentially freak you out, I take no responsibility and make no guarantees that any of this will work and results will vary so much in certain cases that it might generate the opposite response, it is time for you to gather your thoughts and opinion on the subject and test them because at the very least I want you to take away that monsters exist in the daylight and not at night. Those that are close can do the most damage but just do not be like Stalin, who invent photoshop by killing those near him and cutting them out of pictures. Things happen, life changes, learn to change lives and when to change things, that balance will be the guiding light, everything has some form of balance whether we are aware of it or not.

Epilogue

I did not have to write this, but I did because as much as I hate reading, I can string words together like grandma's knitting (in every way). I feel there is no reason to waste this ability. This experience is one unlike any other I have experienced, and I am sure this book is going to bring me more as I age. But if this is successful, I will be writing more content and creating a platform, maybe not a blog or a youtube channel but something unique. My original plan was to start a podcast after this book where I have people with any problems in their life join a call, and we talk it out, and problem solve while you listen, and one of you might be chosen to get your problem solved. That was the plan, and it might still be, but I have to get out and do it. I do not think my method of thinking is new, but I can say it is underrepresented. Not to tute my own horn, but I am very versatile in my thought processes. Based on the problem at hand, there is no one method to solve every problem because then we would not have problems. At the same time, as I age, I do not think I want to be known as an author; it just does not feel right. My other plan was to do a TED talk, but I always forget to write down a topic. With what is happening with the world, I might do an E-TED talk.

www.ingramcontent.com/pod-product-compliance
Lightning Source LLC
Chambersburg PA
CBHW070805050426
42452CB00011B/1902